B
N
P

BEST
NEW
POETS

2024

50 Poems from Emerging Writers

Anders Carlson-Wee, Guest Editor
Jeb Livingood, Series Editor

This book is published in cooperation with *Meridian* (readmeridian.org)
and the University of Virginia Press (upress.virginia.edu).

For additional information, visit us at
bestnewpoets.org
twitter.com/BestNewPoets
facebook.com/BestNewPoets

Text set in Adobe Garamond Pro and Droid Sans

Printed by Lightning Source

ISBN: 979-8-9917112-0-3
ISSN: 1554-7019

Contents

About *Best New Poets*

Welcome to *Best New Poets 2024*, our twentieth annual anthology of fifty poems from emerging writers. At *Best New Poets* we define "emerging writer" narrowly: our anthology only features poets who have not yet published a book-length collection of their own poetry. Our goal is to provide special encouragement and recognition to poets just starting in their careers, the many writing programs they attend, and the magazines that publish their work.

From February to May of 2024, *Best New Poets* accepted nominations from writing programs and magazines in the United States and Canada. Each program and magazine could nominate two writers, and those poets could send a free submission to the anthology. For a small entry fee, writers could also submit poems as part of our open competition. Eligible poems were either published after January 1, 2023, or unpublished. Which means you are not only reading new poets in this book, but also some of their most recent work.

In all, we received a total of nearly three thousand poems. A pool of readers and the series editor evaluated these submissions, sending just under two hundred selections to this year's guest editor, Anders Carlson-Wee, who chose the final fifty poems that appear here.

Guest Editor's Introduction

In 2012, I took the two thousand dollars I'd saved from my work as a personal trainer at the YMCA and booked a one-way flight to Italy. I was twenty-eight and unhappy. I had no prospects. My only plan was to walk across the world, camping each night wherever I could find a tucked-away-enough place to roll out my sleeping bag, until I ran out of money. It was a form of adventure, sure, but also of masochism. Four months later, having slogged across the Dinaric Alps through Croatia, Bosnia, Montenegro, and Albania, I found myself in Greece, too skinny, too sunburned, and freshly robbed.

That day, after the robbery, I took shelter from the ungodly heat in a café and anxiously calculated how much longer I could last on the little I had left. I knew how to do this: in 2009, I'd spent six months bicycling across the United States on two hundred bucks, getting my food from dumpsters; and for all my twenties, I'd lived on three thousand dollars per year. But this was Europe: there wasn't nearly as much waste to prey on here. Maybe if I was careful, if I milked every cent, I could go another half a year. Oh, who was I kidding? My trip was falling apart. My life was falling apart. If only I hadn't been robbed!

Distracted, lost in this wretched headspace, void of all confidence, I offhandedly checked my email. There was a new message from *Best New Poets*. Best New Poets? What was that? I knew what it was, but it seemed so impossibly far away, another language, another life, someone else's life, a wishful thought from a forgotten world that had caught up to haunt me. But why?

Right—I'd submitted a poem before leaving for Europe, and here, now, a lifetime later, was the formal rejection of that poem. More heartbreak.

I opened the email, eager to delete it as soon as I took in the bad news. I read it. Then I reread it. Then I closed it and marked it as "unread" and reopened it and read it again.

It was an acceptance. My first. I'd never been accepted, never been published, not once, not anywhere. But now, it seemed, *Best New Poets* wanted to change that.

When I look back on my writing life, this moment of first acceptance stands out as profoundly consequential. It was a vote of confidence at a time when I so desperately needed one, a time when I was literally wandering the world, hoping—although I did not know it—for direction. I was lost, I was robbed, I didn't belong, despair was overtaking me, and then, suddenly: acceptance. My own personal lodestar. It was the first time I allowed myself to think, Okay, maybe I can really do this. Maybe I can be a writer.

Now, twelve years later, it is my tremendous honor and great joy to be 2024's editor for *Best New Poets*. I have not taken the task lightly: I know how much acceptance meant to me, how deeply I valued what felt like an outstretched hand from the editor, offering to help pull me up a mountain so engulfed in fog that I couldn't even see it, even as I sensed that its face was too steep and too cold to navigate alone. To be in a position where I can be the one offering the hand—I can hardly describe the euphoria.

Yet, for some unknown reason, before I started reading submissions, I worried that there wouldn't be enough standout pieces, that I'd have to reluctantly usher in works I didn't value. The opposite proved to be true. There were so many strong styles, so many wild idiosyncratic voices, that I had to take great pains to narrow it down to the final fifty. Which is to say, buckle up: you're in for a real ride. You're about to play Russian roulette with God. You're about to overdose on fentanyl, then hear an Auschwitz survivor's testimony. You're about to meet a son who protects his aging, stubbornly-still-driving father by massacring his car, then teleport to 1726 as Mary Toft gives birth not to children, but to rabbits. And that's just five of the fifty poems compiled here.

So get going—I won't delay the main show any longer. But just one last note to the poets I've chosen: You are gifted beyond the bounds of any anthology. I only hope this acceptance gives to you even a shred of what it gave to me back in 2012. And in case you don't already feel this way about your extraordinary talent, let me say: You can really do this.

—Anders Carlson-Wee

ANDERS CARLSON-WEE is the author of *Disease of Kings* (W.W. Norton, 2023), *The Low Passions* (W.W. Norton, 2019), a New York Public Library Book Group Selection, and *Dynamite* (Bull City Press, 2015), winner of the Frost Place Chapbook Prize. His work has appeared in *Poetry*, *The Paris Review*, *Harvard Review*, *BuzzFeed*, *American Poetry Review*, and many other publications. The recipient of a fellowship from the National Endowment for the Arts, he is represented by Massie & McQuilkin Literary Agents and lives in Los Angeles.

Rachel Morgan
Motherless Afternoon

There's this wild maple tree I want to tell you about.
The leaves are yellow in the middle and foxy red

at the eave-pointed edges. You're almost too old to care
about this kind of thing, but one day you'll be old enough

to really care about this kind of thing. Later, I bike
into the prairie wind at Ada Hayden Heritage Park.

We almost named you Ada. We almost so many things.
I don't know if every intimacy is gnawed by deceit,

but even now I want to assure you there are many
marvelous things on this earth. The sky is opening up

into the monochromatic season. We tell two
kinds of stories—what we did and almost did.

Afterword, the tailwind helps me bike back home and
everything is easier. I can still feel my legs pedaling

long after I've stopped, the cold zipping through my jeans.
I can rename you, Ada, Ada, Ada. Rename us, me, you, this.

Here, hold out your hand, I'm bringing you back this leaf.
Its absence made more sky. It is one of the marvelous.

Jiordan Castle
Sometimes I Want to Move to the Suburbs

though we don't have any children. Saturday
mornings I want to be in my own fluorescent basement,
cheating a plastic puck through a goal, knuckles
red as a stop sign. I want to swim in a pool
shaped like a kidney bean. I've never opened my eyes
underwater. I blamed the chlorine. Then sharks.
There was always fear to kill my curiosity. What if
no one can tell me the right move, if this is
all wrong, if this is not who I am, or if
this is who I could be, soaked by rain
and saved by sun. Made new, greener in the suburbs.
I can't tell me anything tonight. I can't remember a time
I walked the dog and felt safe in any city,
pick a city. This is a fact, I don't tell myself,
holding my face up to the light, examining one fat pupil,
then the other in the bathroom mirror, looking for signs
of life. I get stranger every year I live away from
the house where I first watched *All Dogs Go to Heaven*.
Ever since, I've been watched by men on train cars
and sidewalks and grocery stores. I want
a G-rated Halloween, just once, to take a fistful of
Butterfingers from a bowl, the fun-size wrappers light
in my palm. I want children with severed heads
to ring my doorbell. I want to know who I am
when I answer.

Perry Janes

Ode to the Landmark Main Art Theater, Since Demolished, in Royal Oak, Michigan

Summer in high school, our few months of Northern heat,
and all my friends and I wanted was to escape back
into our familiar chill, the over-air-conditioned
cinema returning us to our bodies, their winters,
hard edges against the cold, and not, as outside,
bleeding into the night, its humidity absorbing us
into the astigmatism of street lamps
gilding other teens, luckier teens, cruising
down the block to Eminem and D12 or else
pausing in the intersection to kiss—messily,
extravagantly—where the stoplight rouged
their lips when pulled apart, still sticky
with sweat and saliva. My friends and I,
no less fortunate or more average than any
ordinary adolescents confusing loneliness
with desire, would disappear night by night
into the theater's black box, our shoulders
sometimes brushing, or butter-greased fingers
skimming in the shared tub of popcorn
we pooled our allowances to purchase, and
looking back on it now, this was, it must
have been, our first romance. I don't mean
sex, though the question of it hung over
everything, though I try to pretend
that wasn't the case, that we weren't,
like so many others, involuntarily cast
in bit parts of boys barely able to contain

their own want, as when, once, I caught
my high school crush in the hallway
after hours. It was laundry day. I wore
a XXL t-shirt my home-ec teacher had
remarked, earlier, made me *look something
like a drowned rat.* And so, suddenly foisted
before the lens of my own longing, I shrank
away from the audience, here being
a euphemism for the excruciating
60 seconds in which I could not acknowledge
or make eye contact with the girl awkwardly
crossing her Keds in front of me, my gaze
slipping off lockers, windows, and how,
after, my boys spent exactly five minutes
having their fun, clowning my clumsiness,
before clapping me on the shoulders
and steering us, again, to what we sometimes
called *the latchkey matinee.* What I mean is
we understood one another's yearning,
impatient for a future we each imagined
but couldn't yet reach, with no salve or solution
except the screen, tall, lit with melodramas
as sprawling as the restlessness we tried to quell
but couldn't. I would sit, sometimes, aware
of Will's breathing in the dark, Kevin popping
gum beneath his tongue, Mike elbowing
Kevin in the gut, and sometimes, I would crouch-
shuffle my way out to the aisle alone, though
the theater was empty, though there was no one
to hide from but the projectionist I glimpsed
looking down from their windowpane on our small
and silent family, where I would slip into the red

carpeted lobby flanked by velvet curtains,
the concessions stand abandoned by cashiers
playing hooky until the next showtime,
and imagined I had stepped off-frame
into the backstage of my own life,
wondering when one story ends
and another begins.

Mickie Kennedy
Blue Collar

When I asked how electricity worked,
Dad bent down from the cash register
to explain the red and black,

the positive and negative,
the shiny copper of the ground.
Every few months,

he sliced open his hand
stripping wire. *Maybe when you're older,*
he said, *I'll teach you.*

When he sent me to the back
to restock the drink coolers,
I pressed my face against the glass,

so cold it stung my lips.
Later that day, the scrape
of my mop against concrete,

the endless rinsing of dirty water.
The mop-head was older than I was.
With every swipe, it shed strips of cloth.

I crawled on my knees
to pick them up,
to save my dad from bending.

Shop closed, windows dark,
we shared a Coke out front.
I watched the mound of his throat

rise and fall as he swallowed.
The parking lot was gravel,
crushed small and packed.

His dream: blacktop
so smooth we could skate.
He walked his fingers

across my head, pretending.

—Nominated by *The Southern Review*

Shannan Mann
A Bouquet of Lotuses for Your Birthday

1. Lotus feet, lotus hands, lotus eyes, lotus rage.

2. The Kosi embankment's failure was first blamed, in 1968, on rats and foxes.

3. Imagine the river is a tongue.

4. The upper lip basins from southern Tibet and eastern Nepal. The lower lip glaciates to the Ganga, singing to the Himalayan snow leopards and wild yaks.

5. Why politicians do not care for rivers I do not know.

6. To ascribe holiness to a body of water and then to defile the water's body.

7. This is our world, beloved. The world you and I share with our daughter.

8. But the rain, you say. The rain and moonlight freckling the rivers. How she counts seventeen stars! How she gobbles lotus seeds jewelled with pink salt!

9. I want to stay here forever. You there, her there. I—a blue stream cascading, crescendoing, eroding, rebirthing between your two bodies, one child, one man, a family of baby steps.

10. The first time I heard of a lotus was long before the first time I ever saw one, weeks after I had searched for lotuses in the Auckland Botanical Gardens.

11. I was supposed to be selling the *Bhagavad-gita* in the strip malls that day.

12. But after reading so much about lotus this and lotus that and feeling irrevocably melancholic, I just wanted to see the damn flower in real life, you know?

13. I did not find it that day.

14. An alluvial fan, one of the largest in the whole wide world, billows from the Kosi escarpments where, on August 18, 2008—the same day that a suicide bomber drove a car into an Algerian military school killing forty-three people and hurting forty-five, the same day Belarusian weightlifter Andrei Aramnau broke three world records, exactly a month (depending on whom you ask) before the 2008 stock market crash, and exactly (if you ask my mother) two years before my brother was born—heavy monsoon rains submerged all the fields. Countless villages flooded. Many months later, they counted 434 dead bodies but it is difficult to count bones under water.

15. But I am not warning you about the evils of water on your birthday.

16. You who love water.

17. You who drink your water at 69 degrees fahrenheit with a splash of lemon, honey and slivered ginger.

18. You who wish to be water.

19. You because of whom—if we left the other—there'd be no way I could live in Norway or England because of all the rain.

20. No, I am not telling you a crying story. I'm telling you how the farmers of Dhanauri Village got rich off lotuses by harnessing the floodwaters.

21. The same floodwaters that carried ashes became flower beds.

22. The man who broke this news bears your name. First and last.

23. Imagine, Karan, fields of stagnant floodwater simmering with nelumbo.

24. And then the rhizomes gather like hair or fins. The garter-green stems flare brilliant beneath this water of death. The swollen flowerbuds pink, yellow, white, and—rarer than rainbow eucalyptus or the peacock spider or the glowing forests of Japan—blue.

25. Blue lotuses are said to bring children, dreamless sleep, wisdom, a sun-in-your-face-under-snowfall happiness, mad euphoria, religious fervour, cancer cures. They heal the heart, the gut, the genitals, blood.

26. Musk and blue lotus stamen—the Vedas say this is how Krishna smells.

27. The Lord who is a Lotus. From his navel, a lotus stem umbilicals into a lotus whorl, upon which Brahma alights.

28. Utterly lost, alone and confused he turns in all the directions.

29. He finds nothing, but sprouts three additional heads, one for each direction, to long, to lose, to look.

30. Devastated by a universal flood, his lotus home swaying amid the catapult of elements, he begs. He bashes his heads on the lotus carpel. Weeps, though his million tears from his four heads are flooding further the earthless world. Finding a perforated void in the lotus heart, he dives into its body, swimming downstem to reach his origin. He swims for centuries though centuries do not yet exist. Time is not yet born. We are still daydreams glimmering over Vishnu's eyelashes.

31. Defeated, he swims back. Little fish, Brahma, little lord of the Lordless void.

32. What is one to do, beloved?

33. What is anyone to do with a broken world, a broken body, when there is no one left to bind or, if nothing else, to break further with?

34. And then he heard two syllables.

35. All the poems we want to whisper to each other, all the slogans of revolution, all our lonely prayers summed up in two syllables.

36. Your name has two syllables.

37. *tapa*

38. Heat. A child, I lived always with sunlight and water—sweat on skin. Once, running across the road in burning May, I was struck by a motorcycle. Not in the way you might be struck by a poem watching a little girl smell a flower but perhaps exactly in that way. I bled for hours. The blood felt cold though it was meant to be hot.

39. Penance. I'm not sure if not eating grains for a year, not fucking for four, and barely sleeping is penance but if it is I performed it and at the end all I wanted was something like the All Encompassing Blackness to consume me. No wonder no flower is black.

40. Oppression. Not so much by figures of beauty, but I am oppressed often by the thought that I might get exactly what I deserve and that is always a cause for concern.

41. To burn in self-inflicted suffering.

42. To reach the lotus in a cesspool. To reach the Lord in our solitude. To reach love though love be an icicle piercing the heart.

43. The Rig Veda glorified our four-headed Brahma, the creator with a lifetime of 311040 billion human years.

44. Oh, but a few lightning flashes. A candle left to melt in a cow skull. The Koh-i-Noor glittering beneath a confetti of blood on an empty throne.

45. In other words, nothing.

46. Almost.

47. Imagine a field of blue lotuses again. Hush, my penchant for trauma, for gore. Before Anasuya was born, I imagined a bulldozer crushing me. The Holdenian teenager I was, I did not mind. Now, so often—on streets, in trains, by rivers—I am so afraid, jittering, hawk-eyed to ensure she does not fall into a snakepit nestled above a volcano curdling and churning with dragon detritus.

48. Oh, where would we find it? Mothers find fear everywhere.

49. On your birthday, I am imagining how a hundred deaths could have happened. A hundred ways we could have never met. A hundred years of shit and bones in a pond overtaken by an algal bloom— lotusless, zeroed with the cancelled memory of the past perfect.

50. Please, help me yield. Plow my skin, dive into my veins, measure the pieces left behind by everyone that left, and tell me how the moon looks so pure despite all the eyes that envy it. That the Lord offers the first sip of holy water to the devil. That the massacre of one land is a lotus mine for another. That honeybees will find molecules of nectar in crumpled flowers. That we are her parents but she always shushes us to sleep. That the lotus rich farmers gave much of their wealth to help the flooded homeless. That this world of ours is burning, but you have brought a mouthful of cold water and are waiting to kiss me.

Sharon Pretti
Waterline

Count the days of rain: window glass, fence post, tree line.

We lose everything we know about the sky.

I'm not asking to be consoled.

Nights of sleep and finally, the first dream

of my brother. A ballfield flooded and him

alone in the bleachers, looking at me like I hadn't

been wading through water, like I wasn't worried.

I want to know how long a levee can hold

before breaking. A day length, a dream length?

The night I sped to the hospital, I made it

while he was still warm, machine sounds silenced.

I want to know how damage is measured,

entire towns capable of going under.

This is what I remember: my hands curled

around his forearm, the hour it took for him to cool.

—Nominated by *The MacGuffin*

Fiker Girma Negash
Wishlist

I've made a list of things
to tell you once you get out
of jail. The look of rain in early
spring. The country I was
writing, looking for a name
as sullied. In the end, you called
me *Love* instead of *Where*
Jesus left. He was here. Now,
he is not. Mortality is just
like space: unconvincing in any
meaningful way. The difference
between grief & anger: our years
together. There is no justice. Or poetry.
Just life before the will is read
& divine interruption. I could go to any law
school if I applied. This poem,
enough. Only I want to stop
writing about where we are
from as punishment & I could.
But the farmers will keep
tilling. They, the land. Poetry,
nothing. A friend suggested
yoga & I didn't laugh.
So many scars. We are
what we became one day. Mother,
still. You are there, a bright
orange jerrycan for a toilet. After

we buried him, the mourners came
to us, bowing. *Bereaved*
is one name though it says nothing
of the order of hurts. *Wife arrested
for a failed liver*, then *daughter*.
These are the names
impressed on us like nails,
moons against us.

Ann Weil
Moon Child

We drank Tang, just like the astronauts,
but stopped short of breakfasting
on freeze-dried eggs. Saturdays,
Dad melted Crisco in the fryer,
dropped little meteors of batter
into the bubbles, served up fritters
with real maple syrup. Sixties kids
had it made in the shade—all-day freedom
on banana-seat bikes, Oscar Mayer
bologna sandwiches eaten on the fly,
Nestle's chocolate chips folded
into Toll House cookie dough by Mom,
a June Cleaver clone except that she wore
capris instead of a dress, and hair statuesque
in an eight-inch beehive. Her Max Factor lipstick—
Electric Pink—always freshly applied,
the house swept, dusted, and promptly at 6,
martini'd. The family's crisp white edges
began to curl at cocktail hour, threatened to tear
at dinner, the effort of kindness simply
too burdensome for our mission commander to bear.
As the Green Giant canned peas were passed
and the potato-chipped tuna noodle casserole
spooned out, one wrong word, an errant opinion,
an ill-timed sigh—and all planets ceased
rotation around the sun. I sat farthest away,
little brother too close. Little elbows on the table…

a big man can be a fast man. A spoon a weapon.
A woman, powerless. A moon child escapes
in her mind-made spaceship—rocketing away
to the lunar maria, their vast darkness
so perfect for hiding.

Andrew Chi Keong Yim
On Day One, I Quit

On day one, I quit the Cub Scouts.
It was tradition to howl at the end
of each meeting. I refused to howl.

Mom held me in the parking lot.
Inside, the pack whooped and cried,
animal brothers under the moon.

I don't remember if Mom ever got
her deposit back. Across the street,
Sacred Hearts Academy rang its bells

on the hour. The last scene of *Lost*
filmed in their chapel. Light shone
through its arch and a man walked

into heaven. In Illinois, my father
and I spent our only winter together.
I slept on the living room floor

and woke to passing freight trains.
That week refused to carry snow.
Sixty on Christmas, we drove back

and forth through melting suburbs.
He told me about a distant aunty
who'd died suddenly when bitten

by a dog. This was back in China.
I've let this country sit between us.
Its melodramas and indoor malls.

Fields of wheat beset by family cars.
We passed house after bright house
flushed with lights but no sound.

—Nominated by *Washington Square Review*

Perry Levitch
Leporiform

1726: Mary Toft began birthing rabbits
or rather rabbit parts, floppy
pink torsos and little bald legs,
sharp nails intact. Mary miscarried
her fetus, story says, chasing after a rabbit,
her ensuing fascination so strong that
rabbits too started slipping from her
in half-dreamed pieces. now
it's assumed her husband helped
put the dead rabbit pieces inside her,
where she would hold them weeks
at a time. seventeen leporine
miracles. ten royal surgeons peering
into her mystery. the whole country
burrowing. she is whisked away
to a bathhouse outside London
for observation. now it's assumed
Mary first miscarried because peasants
were forced to till the hop fields
all pregnancy long. Mary at rest
only in labor. Mary half-expecting
the kits to nuzzle their way out alive.
three human babies wailing for her
back home, their horrible faces the same
color as the insides of their mouths.
Mary who cannot choose where to pin
the life her body conjures. this is

a prayer for every body bearing
against its will: may what lives
dart free of you, off into the field.

—Nominated by *The Southeast Review*

Dylan Weir
Bambi

There was a balcony overlooking a small pond of black water. By the water, a clearing through which we'd watch the same scrawny deer saunter on its three good legs every morning. Coffee and cigarettes, a few big blue books on the wrought-iron tables between us. The story, as it was later related to us by a counselor or orderly—I can't remember now, was it a nurse maybe?—was that the deer had been hit on the highway some years back. Mangled and seizing like an eel on the median. You see them everywhere up here in the Middle West, animal carcasses decorating the shoulder like an abstract expressionist's canvas. Anyway, the poor old lady who mowed Bambi down ended up calling fish and wildlife or whatever government agency one calls to come clean up such a mess. The deer's hind left leg had been torn clear off. When the park ranger arrived, dressed in his crisp khaki slacks, he decided the best course of action would be to put the animal out of its misery. Returning to the truck for his rifle, I suppose he muttered a few solemn words to himself, or sighed and thought longingly about how he should've taken his father's advice and attended law school instead of having to deal with this horseshit. When he shot the deer, it did not die. He shot it again and again it did not die, but stood and ran to the side of the road. Turning to the lady, he said, *Ma'am, I do believe this animal's made its case.* And so the deer survived. Limping around the campus of an adult drug and alcohol rehabilitation facility. Finding a home amongst the dishonored cops; the petty criminals and the unrepentant felons; the lonely, neglected, and pill-popping housewives of Minnesota and Iowa, Omaha and Olathe. After hearing the story, I remember watching the men of my unit smuggle apples from the cafeteria in the pockets of their sweatpants, shuffling through the line at the nurse's station for our nightly medication, then tossing them into the clearing right before bed, after smoking their last cigarettes.

Isabella DeSendi

My Death Urge Is Strong (Self Portrait at Thirty)

Kait says my death urge is strong—
        that's why I try to sabotage my life.

Far out on the river, boats float from harbor
        to harbor like lovers becoming strangers

becoming lovers once again
        and all I can think about is distance, my mother

and the hunger she carried with her
        before she became American, hunger that spreads

in me like juniper erupting all over the park
        the winter I decide I can't breathe, don't eat.

I'm in a new city now but I'm not lonely. Kait was right
        about my urge but we're not friends anymore.

October again, the engine of summer stopped
        by the galloping trance of an impossible cold

light and certain as the music
        of one hundred blue wings

humming like soft machinery
        in my bones. I thought by thirty I'd stop looking

at my body as a wind-ripped metaphor—
       or would at least have learned to love

my ruinings the way a child loves collecting pennies—
       worth something because they unburied them.

Worth something because they're mine.
       Instead, I order oat lattes every day of the week

and practice laying sentences down in stanzas
       like bodies lying on a bed. These days, I am only writing

to understand the character of myself as an attempt
       to have grace when I fail me.

In here, there is a version of me that never felt
       shame for helping my mom clean offices for cash.

The light is dewy, cinematic. I am inarguably holy
       and never lonely, never cruel. In here, I can recite

the name of every film in Timothée Chalamet's
       repertoire even though Kait told all our friends

that I'm an indie film poser. I don't care.
       This is what life is: intimacy, chance, the thrill of so much

beginning new and so often always its end.
       At the beginning of my mom's new life,

a photo was taken of her blowing kisses
       toward the shore the day she left and never looked back.

I miss the friends I've lost to age, small griefs, love.
      In poems, I can remember them.

In poems, I can believe the person I say I am
      in a story I invent that goes like this: Bella waits

by the water when a dog, loose from its leash,
      runs up to her ecstatic, demanding to be acknowledged

as the living often do—yes, I decide
      the plot will start here: the animal bounding toward her.

Its face held between her palms
      the way only strangers' faces can hold the mystery

of one another. For just a moment, this trust.
      Eyes linked having understood

the wildness that rests between them.
      But before you think of me as hero, know this:

I knew my mother was hungry
      and I still took food from her plate.

The dog returns to its owner as it must.
      I don't save anyone

but I blow kisses to all the strangers
      passing by me on small boats. Nothing else

but a blue sail on the water
      growing smaller in the distance.

Chris Ketchum
Fentanyl

It was like being underwater,
he says, for so long you forget

you're drowning. He slumped
in the driver's seat of his sedan,

bass beating in the Blue Ridge
dark. Down, then further down.

A partygoer pounded on his window.
She tried the door, found Narcan

in his glove compartment.
I don't believe in God, he says,

but that was God. Rubbing
the red back of his wrist

where the cuff rides up.
I don't tell him I still see

the fearless boy inside him
who I used to know—

What I say is You know better
than to count on God.

Once I met a surfer who wintered
in a Portuguese fishing village

as he waited for the perfect swell.
When he finally caught

a seventy-footer, the slope was
too steep, the chop too rough

to control. You aim for the edge
of the shadow but the break

outruns you. You're falling, he said,
and praying to master the fall.

Emma DePanise

Waterspout

A cloud begins to fill the wind and spins
          on warm and waiting water. Air forgets
its roots. A spiral spraying over fins
          and plastic. Maybe we're becoming less

and less. Tornadic waves I want to hold.
          A little damage is enough. The eye
is drawn to shore, to windshields, first cars sold
          to teens. The vortex of this humid sky

is leaking. Take a picture, look away
          again. We've made a ligature of spit
and seaweed. Lightning strikes across the bay
          and ducks go under water. See the slit

of sun through clouds that shimmer back to sleep
          and how we left our sweat and steps on streets.

*

Tornadoes are rare in Maryland but try and stop them. June, 2009, on the Chesapeake Bay and a funnel downs from a cumulus cloud to brush the water. Stone clouds. I was in middle school at your house and the air is rising and rotating on a vertical axis. We were probably painting canvases or laying out in our bathing suits. Our birthdays a day apart but not in this season. You wanted me to join the swim team. Wind direction shifting, the bay breeze blew and the storm moved from Anne Arundel County to over the bay. Your parents went to church and mine didn't. My mom protested the elementary school administration and yours wouldn't let you buy a rainbow-colored backpack for school. 3:52 p.m. and the storm passed a little north of Love Point, where you lived, just a mile's walk from the beach. We didn't see the spout but heard about it after. When the wind swirled and the sky darkened and thunder shook the emptiness of our stomachs, we went outside. The rain was hard and fat and heavy on our bodies. We jumped up and down and circled your yard. Lightning lit up your face. You didn't have a pool so this was the next best thing. Dark spot to spiral pattern to spray ring to vortex. Finally, decay. We'll tell other people about *the rush* of dancing during *practically* a tornado. Later, we won't hang out for years, until we're at the same college. Followed by another stretch of silence. 4:10 p.m. and the storm has dissipated over the Chester River, no damage reported.

*

Try to hold still within the wild
                breath of wind and moisture. You are
just beginning to fly and flail
      with silverfish and minnows losing their

breath. Of wind and moisture, you are
         trying to stay whole. Dip under water
            with silverfish and minnows losing. There
is a softness in the eye the color of light

trying. To stay whole, dip under water
         into algal blooms. Their green film
             is a softness. In the eye, the color of light
swirls. Ask it to rain you down on another town, thunder

into algal blooms. Their green film
           tries to hold. Still within the wild
swirling, ask it to rain you down. On another town, thunder's
      just beginning to fly and flail.

—Nominated by the University of Missouri Creative Writing Program

Andrew Navarro
Heroes, Villains, Clouds

General Santa Anna
years after losing his leg
to the French at the battle
of Veracruz had his leg dug up
and reburied with full
military honors. To salvos,
poetry recitals, and touching
speeches, Santa Anna wept
as they lowered his limb
encased in a crystal container
into the Earth. Weeping
so softly he transformed
into wind. His uniform,
with its swaying tassels,
left abandoned in a chair.
Today, there is not a single cloud
in the sky. They have all been buried
in the fields beside the fattening
crops. Given time the clouds will grow
into the heroes and villains of another
generation. Heroes and villains born
in towns much like the one
I am walking through;
where a young man stands
before the baker's daughter,
his hat held in his hands,
and a butcher scrubs blood

off rubber aprons and gloves; blood
and white foam mixing
in the street gutter a drunk
inadvertently steps in, his barefoot
caked in mud. En la calle San
Sebastián where statues keep vigil
of pigeons and a shattered glass bottle
contemplates the day. I could say
I am map of what we were;
a thousand years condensed
into a breath. How between
each joint in my body
lies a space as dark and cold
as the soil in a field of grass
where the bodies of soldiers lay,
their eyes reflecting the sky.
Place your ear to my chest
and listen—
the field of grass
rippled by wind.

Nathan Metz
Fragment Sonnet

In Larry Rivers's *Washington Crossing the Delaware*
time smears like the knees of a man running
towards his burning home, tripping,
weeping, getting up, weeping, running,
weeping, tripping again, weeping, and finally
crawling that quick cracked crawl
in an otherwise soundless
and snow-softened night.

—

No no no. I think it was lipstick.
Time smears like lipstick under your nervous thumb.

—

And that is something else history does:
yesterday I remember doing three things.
Last year, maybe seven.

—

In Emanuel Leutze's version
(in high school history textbooks—
gold frame around old oil, shining)
Washington stands at the bow
of yesterday straight

as a promise, clear
as a lie.

—

In the dustiest corner of the basement,
a blank canvas from the week
I wanted to be a painter has lost
its mind, spewing nonsense, coughing
cobwebs. I don't have the heart
to throw it away. It wouldn't let me
sleep last night, whispering
yes-ter-day-yes-ter-day-yes-ter-day
like a child learning the Latin names
for poisonous flowers, and cackling
like a letter ripping itself in a gutter.

—

Simile is the language of history.
"This is like that is like this is like that"
and after a while, and with great
concentration, you can finally hold
a war in your hands. This is supposed
to be a good thing.

—

When I was nine, I remember
peering out the backseat
and glimpsing poppy flowers
blooming by the freeway.

—

There is no theory of color,
the canvas once declared after a week
so quiet I forgot about art. *But*
there are two commandments.
The first commandment is

—

and the second commandment is
"Thou shall not let the first commandment
kill thee fully, or at least
silently."

—

A brushstroke, too, can't run from simile.
Touch is like this.
It can last this long.
It will leave a mark, like that.

—

Blurriness is the only product of conflict.
One thing (a boy, a paintbrush,

a general) can't see just ahead
and moves terribly fast. The other thing
(a flower, a nothing, a gun)
can't see just behind

—

and stays right here, close, still, still
enough to be considered, considered
and forgotten.

—

I struggle but can't remember the color.
I mean, they were orange, but

—Nominated by *Santa Clara Review*

Casey Patrick

Fern

Minneapolis, summer 2020

Now I've dreamed of the deer in the cemetery so often, I worry
she isn't real. I pace my bedroom, following her hooves
sinking into soft, mowed grasses. In my nights, she sleeps
in open graves and feeds on the flowers people leave
on flat stone. Through winter, she greets me at the gates.
I have never tried to touch her. These days, I prepare
my loneliness like a room. Only the ordinary terrible things
have happened to me. Someone tells me
her name is Fern. These days, my loneliness
is everybody's loneliness. She didn't leave
when our city was on fire. Or maybe
we both came back. I weigh *tame* against *good*
on the polished scales. Fern is tending the graves,
treading a desire line from one to another in the dark.

Avia Tadmor

My Grandfather Delivers a Survivor's Testimony at Yad Vashem

My first name was Adolf. My father,
my mother, what did they know?

From the German, meaning both *noble*
and *beast*. Meaning they trusted I'd live

unafraid my roots could be showing,
less worried that someone will see

through to the part of me
longer than my own life.

I have three names, four tongues, a place
behind my heart where I carry

my earliest dead. I was fourteen.
The ID my father's friend forged for me

said I was a Catholic farmboy. Meaning I'd learn
to bury the parts of me that I had once

named my life. On Sundays, I'd join
the old couple in church. Under the sign

of the cross, I'd survey the pews,
boot-marks on every floor tile.

I was a boy. My sister, my brother,
my parents, their parents,

were ashes in October sky. Other Sundays,
I'd imagine the altar-side foyer

leads to a stucco-tiled kitchenette
where my sister sits, peeling lemons.

Or I'd imagine all of them, feeding
on pine nuts out in the snow. Or I'd imagine

they were the snow, crowning
the Tatras. I turned sixteen

on the refugee boat. The ID I found
when we passed through Marseille

said I was married, had fathered
two sons. The first time I held

a Jaffa orange I made a promise: to stay
forever close to land. I studied

phytology, developed a strain of peanut
that can be grown in the cruelest drought.

I knew what hunger was. I didn't know
there are parts of a man that are reborn

with each of his daughters. Mine, three unscathed
coins I'd hold up to the light

with mud-covered hands. If not love, what I felt
for the ground-nuts could be

kinship: the fruit must grow into itself
wholly underground. I don't know how long

before a new geography becomes a home.
Maybe only when you have daughters

who know there will be a permanent plot
of earth they could visit one day,

trace your name on the granite and sing
their grief for you. I chose my new name, Abraham.

Meaning, between beast and nobleman,
I don't trust either. And I knew sacrifice.

I still don't know lucky from fated. Or what
is deserving. What I know is I lived.

Karan Kapoor
My Father Could've Been a Bullet if He Found a Pistol

When I was nine years old my father broke
the walls of our windowless home to hand
me the sky. He brought me trees that vanished,
clouds that bronzed, rivers that thickened
into tar. His manic urge to offer me joy
was like receiving love letters from a volcano.
I did not want him to give. I wanted him
to give up. Alcohol not the scab
but the blade he used to peel the scab.
How easy in ink to alter tense.
How easy to link *victim* with *witness*. A gift
box of rats and false promises. He smuggled
rain, waltzed with fire. A man is rich, he'd say,
by how he gives not how much he owns.
I demanded back the space his kindness colonized.
He chipped the ceiling to reveal the moon
staring like a comma. This was us then,
two train wrecks, two shadows, too long
gone beyond the myth of breast milk,
pearls in tapwater, prayers trapped in fossils.
I am getting to the place where I mistake metaphor
for resolution. Isn't this the easy way out?
If the language we dream in is the real mother,
then the language we wish someone dead in
is a rabid dog. Forgiveness will cost
us everything. Somewhere, I am still
nine. Waiting. Invisible, his will to return

on time. Invincible, our fear. Home, still
a symphony of wounded pigeons.
Somewhere between song and ear, morse
code of love. Buried in this wasteland
with light loaned from tomorrow's sun.
He will put down the bottle. He will?
Why itch, he says, for something forgettable
as time? Life is a line from will to fate, womb
to earth, fog to father. And all lines
are made of infinitesimal circles.
Let the end of your book lie
I have healed. It will be as though
I have healed.

Arielle Hebert
Extra Life

The stray bullet comes through his open window.
I'm seventeen, riding shotgun in my brother's car.
It passes in front of his face.
Did you hear that? he asks. I don't
hear anything, put a hand to my head,
say, *I think I've been stung.* Then—red.
He sees it, everywhere. Grabs a sour beach towel
from the backseat, holds pressure. Cut to
trill of fluorescent lights in a hospital room.
The doctor describes what would have happened
if I'd been hit one inch lower,
in my temple. He asks me to imagine
using a cantaloupe for target practice.
This is the closest I've ever felt to our planet,
to becoming it. Because we must die,
I've stopped biting every silver coin
a stranger presses into my palm,
forget the invisible force telling me
I'll end up like my mother someday.
If there is anything godly out there,
beneath my bravado, I hope
I've been enough, but I will not splinter
my knees proving it to anyone.
Borrowed time. An extra life
to get me to the final boss.
Another chance.

An untethering, serene letting out to sea.
A tendril clipped and carried away
in a pocket to a new garden.

Kaylee Young-Eun Jeong
Last Spring

The same year I starved myself I tried
to sleep with someone new and older
each week, and my mother told me
about citrus trees: how they can sense
when they're about to die, and begin
to flower desperately, the fruit already overripe
before it hits the ground, the inside rotten
as it bursts open—the body, when hungry,
swells, and all that year I looked so full
of a nothing that longed to be enough, standing
on a scale in someone's cramped bathroom
to find I weighed as much as I did
when I was twelve, then having no choice
but to leave the bathroom and fuck him and then
someone else and so on, the way as a child
I didn't know how to draw faces or hands
so all my people had no choice but to be born
with their heads buried in their folded arms,
the way gravity pulls a fruit to the ground and splits it open
like a sentence, as though the dying tree were trying
to leave nothing unsaid, which is why I told my mother
about that year and she answered
with a nature fact, to show me, I guess,
she and the world already knew how the story went,
looking at my body how I might have looked
at my own hunger, if it could have stood
outside of me, ashamed, and begged me

to let it back in, or maybe like she was
the thing not allowed in, my body
a burning house that, before it belonged
to a blank and inexorable fire,
had once been hers.

Lauren Crawford
Galveston

That Houstonian swamp, intimate with the gulf
and her cries, shurling and foamy, the pocket beds
of seaweed peppered with July picnic garlands

and hollow firework shells, Hennessey bottle shards
that gleam brighter than nail polish glaze. They stud
the beach that I, so many, many times, have chosen

as an escape from pitiful fights with my parents
or lying boys, or even my own depression, hollering
at gulls nipping at perch gills braided with bright fishing

twine, each bloody seam opened wide like a hand fan.
There was the gleaned shore, hours before sunrise, its spoils
of the night—toothed conches and whole gritty sand dollars—

stowed fresh on every tourist shelf of the bay in neat rows
all labeled *ocean novelty*. There was my collection of oyster
shells pre-shucked by the wide veins of jetty parting

the major port like long, sharp fingers stretching
into the gulf, waiting to shake hands with the ocean.
There was the warm prickle of sea spray behind my knees

and the rip current tumble dirtying my hair after a plunge.
I want the pink and orange sky nestled atop the sun
and bay like settled wine tannins. I want the sheer mist

of gulf roils lain on me like a mother's dense kiss.
Sinful reams of starlight rooting me in the sandshift;
the Atlantic's everchanging nook. Give me the pelicans

sunning on rotting dock posts infested with algae, waiting
for the skittish minnows to ripple the surface. Give me
the open dark water ready to ambush oil rigs or breed

hurricanes the shape of bad secrets. Give me waves
the color of age itself, let me gulp the salt-stained air
after I've carved my name again into the crumbling deck

rail of the wharf like I own the ceaseless swell of barnacle
teeth and mullet leap, like I could look at the foaming
lips closing over the gannets diving for shrimp knowing

that even if I swallowed the world whole in one massive gulp,
offer my open throat, I would still be starving for more.

Jaz Sufi
Magic Trick

A golden shovel after Jonterri Gadson's "Advice"

When I was a child, my father couldn't decide if he was either
a father or also a child. My mother was a mother's mother. A
woman who knew how to stay. She knew not to look a good
man in the mouth, but she counted each of Dad's teeth when that man
came home late. He was quick to floss away the evidence, but he never
fooled her. She knew all his tricks & tells—late night walks
& early morning meetings, all while he hid other women behind
him like a magician's second deck of cards. If you met him, you
would never guess what cruelty he was capable of, or
how much of it my mother could contain. If you
asked my father if he loved his wife, his family, he'd never
say no. *No* was a woman's word. Before I even learned to stand,
I knew Dad loved me, but I soon learned there was nothing behind
that love. Dad loved the idea of loving us. He reaped a
father's harvest from the neighbors, devoured all their good
graces, but in truth, he was a cardboard cutout of a family man.

And yet years later, he had an accident—cracked his skull as if
it was a bell, & my father awoke a changed man. I
know it sounds like some sitcom scenario, a story he could
spin for someone's sympathy, but no. Suddenly, Dad couldn't recall
why he was standing so far away from his family, or where
he'd left all his grievances. He renewed his apologies to my
mother with words from his own heart, not that of his father.
By then, we were too tall to be carried on his shoulders, but he stood
taller, too, like a lighthouse & less like a cliff. When
my brother & I talk about him now, we call him New Dad. New Dad, he

bought binoculars. Knows all the backyard birds by name. He told
me about them last time I went back home—we sat outside, me
& New Dad, & each time a new song limned the silence, I'd
listen to him instead, & when he asked *Did you know…?* I'd pretend not to know.

Mia Nakaji Monnier
Where I'm From

My mother calls me often on her commute.
Miia, she cries like a bird,
a falling tone.

My mother cries like a bird and I imagine her
in her little white car tracing the coast,
north in the mornings, south at night.
Past the bakery where my youngest brother worked after college,
past the long-gone ice cream shop where I worked in college,
past the surf we each walked separately when we were restless
from the cliffs to the pier,
crushing kelp bladders beneath our heels,
injuring softly, pressing into salt.
Past the paved route we followed as a family,
my brothers taking turns pushing our mother from behind
like the engine of a train.

My mother says, *Time rules all.*
She says, *People try to live too long these days.*
She says, *When I'm dead, I'm dead.*
As in, it's pointless to remember, to ask questions, to memorialize.
Nothing makes me want to fight time like my mother,
her bird cry, the soft, thin skin of her hands,
which hold mine again now that I'm grown,
now that I'm about to be a mother.

My mother touches my belly and I say,
Sawaranakutemo iiyo
You don't have to touch it
but later that day she does anyway,
hesitantly, apologetically.
It's okay, I say and reach out to touch hers.
It's meant to be a joke but it almost breaks my heart,
touching my mother's belly.
That's where you're from, my husband says
when I tell him later.

Where I'm from fog hangs low to the earth,
a watery nest, curved like a bowl, both rugged and soft.
Where I'm from time moves slow as rock,
a shifting of plates, a skittering of clay down cliff to the sea.

M.K. Foster
Of lights that goe before you

> *There is also a kind of light that is seen in the night season and seemeth to goe before men,*
> *or to follow them, leading them out of their way into waters, and other dangerous places.*
> —*William Fulke, 1563*

In a field in the night season, I pray the animals
        away. *Get along now, git*—hoping to God nothing
gets me like it got the children of that far-off
        mother-creature wailing into dark, yet to learn
her babies all been eaten or hit: whatever happens
        in a night field stays between you and the field.
And the night. Hear me out: even fields need
        a god at night. Sharp yowls in crashing grasses,
wild for mercy or silence. Guts rot-ripped as
        over-ripe berries in August: they were beautiful,
all them soft little skin sacks caught, almost
        conceived by the headlights, the gleaming teeth:
all swerve and strike. Surely, even the blow was
        birth, a falling into being, the poor meatlings,
snaggled over mossy clearings, crisping in the road—
        My darling, from one ruined womb to another,
this world is a hell of a lot smaller than we think.
        Turns out, however you enter this life or leave,
the punchline is always having a body, which is
        wearing your own dying. Like it's so easy, like
if it's so easy, prove it: kill yourself, God. Again.
        This time like a mother. Thrashing grasses, hollow
eyes thirsty as smashed glasses: even God needs
        a god at night. That's why light came first—can't

you just see him? Clawing through void, horrified
        by nothing? Can't you just hear the black wind
whistling through the dark holes in his hands?

Michael O'Ryan
Wyoming, February

We spread a picnic blanket on the ice
at the frozen reservoir

as a hockey player kneeled to tie the lace
on his sister's skate.

In accordance with cowboy superstition,
a horseshoe was nailed above the door

at the county library. As you stood
cast in winterlight

among the bright encyclopedias,
I realized my affections

were not unique. Snowflakes
sounded against the windshield

while you read about beekeeping
in tropical climates.

Alcova. Medicine Bow.
Sheep constellated

near a yellow barn
to the sound of late traffic.

Driving past two ghost towns, a fading
scent of vanilla, your hair

draping my shoulder. An abandoned ski lift
loomed in the distance, where its rumored

a bride once lost her corsage
in a summertime avalanche.

Rob Greene

To the Young Second Lieutenant Standing behind Me in Line

At the Keesler AFB Post Exchange in 1987
(Biloxi, Mississippi)

No one looked after me or my brother back then, no CPS,
no Social Workers, the SP's couldn't be trusted,
the off-base cops even worse.

When the P-EX mini-mart clerk told me
I wasn't supposed to be there
and had to leave my Pork & Beans

and bread on the counter, you caught up to me in the parking lot,
my items in your tote bag.
I got caught stealing a sleeved stick of butter

the week prior, but today had returned
with the Susan B. Anthony dollar coin I found in the gutter.
All I had was that and my pocketknife for opening cans and gutting fish,

the reason my privileges were revoked.
I wish I had answered your questions—*What's going on?*
Why can't you shop here? Where are your parents?

before darting off into the night with the can and bread,
dropping the piece of money at your feet.

Sherah Bloor

Canto 33

From an apartment window, Reed watches the dead
leaves spiral under the streetlight then rest. "Focus
now, focus. Remember" he says to himself. "If I could
just recall it, I could make myself into a wormhole. I
could come back to here." Undine rolls over, places
her hand against the cool surface of the motel wall,
"it breathes" she thinks, or "I just feel my life rever-
berate. No. Something still more alive has *its* hand
on *me*" Undine thinks "on my cheek, at the jugular,
It pulls me by my hair." "It pushes me on. It reaches
in. There's no way to stop it, to start again." "I am
a wall, a mirror." Still by the window, Reed now can-
not remember. "Anyway, the world is ending now"
Samara says. "I want to be alone" Graham thinks. He
can't speak, breath rattles in his larynx, "this woman,
she still grips my hand, she'll outlive me as will duty."
"She must sleep though, then I can do it. Die." "If
the world's ending tomorrow" Samara thinks "I'll
walk the white-pebbled path that looks at night to be
floating. I'll wear a silver dress with daisy chains."
"It was as if" Ehud explains "even God prayed for
me then." "But I don't even know" Gillian thinks
"how jasmine looked, as if the scents floated from
off their own aspect." "That's how time got creation
moving, maybe." "I won't be able to get back to that
moment if I can't even remember it." Reed thinks.
"We can't go anywhere that's not a place" Sergei says.

"But there was a movement" Mercia says "the right
to be forgotten." "There were signs. There was chanting."

"But there's no hinge to turn around on" Undine rolls
over again "this life can't be like a rope. It doesn't
grow from my crown, taut. I don't dangle down."
"Not that, something intimate, something flat like
skin is" she thinks. Paula holds her palm over Joy's
mouth "you can't go." "But time. Time and eternity
must be concordant." Sergei swigs some antifreeze,
turns from Czar to lecture a radiator. "Even if" he
says "you imagine opposition as two terms in space,
they are still in space. Contradictions connect just by
contradicting. You can't get out of it." "I know you'd
rather be alone." Lydia thinks "but up until your last
breath, Graham, I won't allow it." "She looks at me"
Kate thinks "looks as if the animal in her is about to
speak." "What's it to perceive? Is it to gouge, burrow,
or weave?" Philip leans over Shamal "insects screw in-
to, suck onto reality, or cling." Phil brushes his lips
lightly to Shamal's temple. Kate thinks, "creature wants
a wet and blinking eye. She wants herself in the image
of a human in here." Kate takes Mae as if "I can drag
her into an adult's body." At the bus station, Ziva
thinks "had two people shared an experience ever,"
thinks, "let me be in my body now, let me breathe."
"Where're we going?" "Places are everywhere." A doll
hangs off Mae's good arm. "There was a movement."

"We've conducted ourselves" Sujita reads "like beings,
like beings with names." Shira asks her father if she
killed God, because Tom said his dad said that she did,

but she cannot remember doing it. Ian pushes a trolly
cart containing carcasses through the deserted village.
"I could pick up sanitizer not eyedrops and hurt myself.
I want to hurt myself, but it's as if I'm not allowed."
Pam can't decide what sounds worse *we are never
alone* or *we are entirely alone*. It takes three men to
hold Konrad down. He's shouting "there is something
wrong." Hakim asks "do you think you're better
company for your dead son than God? It's shameful"
"I'll sanitize the surfaces" Aggi says "nothing's wrong."
Jules runs across the footbridge—she's scared her body
might jump. "I can help" Raul says. "I can help, I can save
you." "There are animals humans will be judged by." "Which?"
"Which species?" The boy shakes his head, Amon doesn't
know species. Lorca's hands are cupped under the faucet.

She hears gurgling in pipes, but no water's coming out,
thinks "you can't know the secret wish your heart makes."
"Don't leave, you've only just arrived" Raul says. "Wali's
here, I pretend," Tessa turns to talk to him "I talk to you.
I force you to see me, alone." "Do you feel it from afar?"
"No, that would be a nightmare. You would have to hover
over my shoulder, invisible. No, God wouldn't allow it."
"What am I doing, I am guilty. For what? For the good
life I've lived, and I've lived it." "We've enclosed ourselves
in, don't you think?" "We fan inward to disappearing points."
"There's a framework for that" Iman offers her client,
"Oblivion, you can use it to blacklist links, but it's not
finetuned or scalable." "The problem is so many things

happen and all the time." Ilona thinks, when the men
touched her, her skin must've touched them back, she

doesn't want to have touched them. There's no other
way. That's how it is. "No, you're filament of my mind.
Dust swirling up like dust devils rise in the dust basin.
They seem spirits, too. We keep seeing them. Faces
in foliage. Figures in clouds. In my dreams, it is me
watching you, in your Netherland's flat" Tessa asks,
"who're you to me?" "God, I just wanted you to want me."
"But they forgive one another" Lucian thinks "when
they have no right. They go together under roofs,
say "so sorry," "never mind," and "no matter." "How
can he make me real if he is not?" Tessa asks "I am
really rather ripped right now" Dylan tells a date. "Oh,
what is it, this thing" Eugene must know what it is.

"The furniture just gets rearranged, that's all that ever
happens here" Sergei projects his voice over Czar's
barking "and instead of freedom, they were given
deliberation." He sits back on his blue milk crate, "it'd
have been too complex otherwise." "Problems in meta-
physics. And this?" He nods, is adequate." "I am the
chosen one," Robert yells, "I've survived everyone,"
"Ok" Dean tells himself "I did it. I raped. I took her
from the Christmas Party to the second storey, I took
her over the tiles, and into a stall." "I did it, but still, I
can't think I am *bad*. Not really, not seriously." "In this
mirror, these ears are still the ears that stuck out under
my school cap. I'm so loveable. I really am. How to be

evil?" Paula realizes, after all, she's no longer afraid of
damnation. It would just be in the order of things and
she's liked everything here so much. "But we must
isolate it down now. Concentrate it. Cut it like a gem

to inspect it from its every single facet." "But what is *it*?"
"*the thing*?" "Despite this damned brain fog, I am going
to flesh it out" Eugene thinks. "These little critters. Not
even human yet" Mark explains "crawled under the earth
through narrow passages for hours just to bury their dead
in a chamber." "It doesn't make sense, but that's what
happened here." Hakim says "if we stopped sinning,
God would just destroy this world and recreate it."

Dominique Ahkong
Witch of the East

The Wicked Witch of the East is
killed as the tale begins—we don't get
to see her face. To face the plots

that landed on me, I kept tapping
my red velcro sneakers together. It
felt closer to practice than magic—

Do you play the violin?
     No. But do you know I tried
to embrace my wickedness? Slurped

that bittersweet black potion of roots,
red dates, and seeds, believing it
would flesh me out. Slipped

into a cheongsam that shimmered
ruby and learned two tones to echo
back to men on the street.

And do you know I tried to efface my
wickedness? Slouched into an *s* and
kept my head down, made the sign

of the cross before biting into my
Marmite and margarine sandwiches.
Wrote in the margins with invisible ink—

I didn't know white ink would show itself
in our equatorial air. When one letter
disappears, *east* can become *eat*.

Before my great-aunt died,
she asked for lanti ek diri.
Black lentil soup and basmati rice.

There are no Munchkins in this story.
The only cyclone my people speak
of is Carol. After the storm,

my mother ate *fist cakes* that
sank in her stomach and my
father swallowed pithi.

    Dear brain, help me—
why must I anglicize everything?
        But what was your baby language?

Do you know that when my
parents say someone's *in China* they
mean they're fast asleep?

       —Nominated by *Fugue*

Bertha Isabel Crombet
Big Bang

I wish I knew how to explain to my mother
that the universe is infinite,
but I'm not as articulate in Spanish,
although it's my first language and my last,
the one whose hand I'll die holding,
offering my regrets the same way
warmth radiates from a wound.
And my mom's English never got
much better than "Yes" & "Thank you,"
the odd, "This is my favorite" and,
"You are very tall" when speaking
to my American boyfriend, who was.
Although everyone is to her, standing
at five feet even on a good day,
depending on the wind. She's done well,
you know, although I never tell her.
She came to this country at forty-three,
speaking more Russian than English,
her life a map folded into tiny innumerable
shapes. In an effort to erase the poverty
she was born into, cleaning is what
she does best. Every mirrored wall weaponed
with a million resplendent reflections.
Every inch of shower tile dried
after every shower to keep the old ghosts away,
good & dead & still wandering through
that old, holed house of her past.

So, she's never been able to
understand anything I say, or me,
the labyrinth of my thoughts
checkered in land mines, each desire
like a leper's caress. So, when I visit
over the summer and we get into a fight
about me not wiping down the counters,
I try to tell her in my best Spanish
about Carl Sagan and our pale blue dot,
that there are more stars in the universe
than grains of sand on Earth, that when
the James Webb telescope released
its first images, I wept with relief
at my insignificance, that when you stare up
in the black onyx of the sky,
you are staring into eternity,
glinting & material & alive.
That nothing really matters, certainly not
cleaning & countertops & the fact
that I wear too much black.
Without answering, she runs her finger
over the Formica surface, the gnarled marble
like the faces of the long dead,
her opinion relentless & intact,
"Mira," she shows me. "Dust."

Michael Mark
Devotion

Because no tools can be carried on the plane,
I buy them at the Home Depot near his apartment

and sneak into my father's building through
the Service Only entrance. Dad's Ford has more dents.

Half hanging fender. He got lucky with the parking spot—
a few steps from the elevator. I puncture the tires

with the spike. Then pick the trunk's lock and stab
the spare. I hear him tell me, when he's driving,

he feels like 50. You drive like you're 95, I say in a laugh
because he's 96 and I'm afraid to be direct. He takes it

as a compliment. I wedge the hammer claw into the seam—
unintentionally scraping some paint—jimmying-up the hood.

I cut all wires because I know how iron-willed he is, and pour
the bag of sugar into the gas tank, crack the windshield

and headlights, pound the battery until the thick clips snap.
I know he's fought all his life for everything so the leftover

Coke from the airport goes into the brake fluid.
Because he taught me integrity, I write a note in big enough

block letters so he can read it even with his double vision.
Of course, I sign it. But don't ask. I will not tell you

what it says. He taught me loyalty, too.

River 瑩瑩 Dandelion
Ghazal Remix for Holy Summers

when i first called my dick, my dick, i trembled.
blushed. stood taller. realized i was becoming more like Jesus.

at Riis, one summer, an older woman asked
if she could suck my Jesus, & i said, Holy—

one summer, my friends & i took our binders off
in the ocean, submerged. felt like jellyfish, Divine,

let five-foot waves wash over us. one summer,
i snuck away from home & stayed in a Temple

in Brooklyn, blazing red room with a lover who showed me
what alchemized in our bodies, never written for Scripture.

in high school, my best friend stood by the Belt & told me
i'd make the perfect boyfriend, if only i were more like God,

a man. i blushed, said i felt the same way about her.
we laid next to each other in bed & spoke of our Holies,

how we precipitated typhoons. i became the boyfriend
i always wanted. called my dick, my dick. recycled the Bible

one summer, i walked the woods alone upstate
to get away from the noise, the dying, to seek Refuge

in Pine Meadows. i crept past the 'no swimming' sign
pulled my shirt off, tucked it away, & dove   into the Kingdom

that could hold me. the water bugs & minnows parted
Heaven for my return, welcomed my name, Holy.

Daniel Schonning
That They Are There

Earth's magnetic field turns over once every three hundred thousand years
and the dead will be here when it does. They nestle deeper in their graves
so as not to scare the deer. Some things are illusory, lose their forms
when looked at from up close—the dead are like that. Heaven and fog and ash
trees are like that, too. Of course, these are precisely the things we can't help
approaching. One morning you walk towards what looks like heaven and end up
drenched, your new blue sweater cold as tin. Cotton dries slowly, if at all.
The deer might be illusory too, but I've never been close enough
to know—you'd have to ask the dead. A predicament. You say: *Which way
is north?* and the dead pretend not to hear. Their field is not magnetic—
it's bottlebrush, ryegrass, and clay. Instead of "north" and "south," all of it
is either "above" or "beside." In the next three hundred thousand years
when the field turns over, every other thing will do the same: tree roots
will turn to canopies, feet to wings. Some things are turning already.
You say: *Which way is Heaven?* and the dead stare up at you like children
quieter than before.

Gabriel Fine
Brain Scan

Ever since, I've been looking for a panacea, eyes
to the irradiating light, hidden

partitions in translucent
gray. Blood-let mind, matter

or lack—limpid facts
I couldn't register. Half in shadow even

the doctor's face. Unable to see thus I saw
floridly, the hemispheres furling

like wings, like so many wings
in a child's drawing. *Eyespot, inkblot*. So swift

this flight to metaphor. *Arabesque*
and *damask*. The images made it

bearable, then forgettable, like an old city
with a stricken name. Impassable routes

of the doctor's hands across the livid map.
This, too: dead region a past

cartography: mother on the Negev, father
a young man dancing under disco glint

in a bunker in the newest territory.
Superimpose the inward country

over the country and the lesion
is transfused, a border craters

out of a border. How many of us are marked
by the radial scar? Each time I nod to the guttering

candlelight what's murdered in my mind.
In the atlas of years the land

shrinks and shrinks, the wound heals
and we forget the wound. Dad's better

now, thank God. Following the news
with us with our brutalized eye. What do I owe

to pain? How to let the image live
but live. Lemon trees

without rubble: a first map. I want to bow
there, color the gray with color. Not

let each day death erase more and more
my sight. Annul memory. In one canto,

Arnaut Daniel tells Dante to *remember,*
when the time is fit, my pain. Utters it

from the flames to which he's damned.
I always thought it cruel, that parting

in tears. He's alive, in the poem,
but barely. Go further, even further back:

there's no language for this damage.
There is a country

named Palestine. I can see its shape, bound
in waters. River, sea, lapping, changed. Can see too

Jerusalem, clot and jewel of the eye.
The years have unmade yet not unmade you.

—Nominated by the Michener Center for Writers

Carson Wolfe
While Wishing She Was Dancing to Kate Bush

The tips are worth the men who
ask her real name, touch her
against the rules.

When her song finishes,
she gets down low on the stage,
uses pointed acrylics to rake

her cash into one pile.
This is the most intimate part.
Not a care how she looks doing it.

Naked except for that cheap pink
wig. When a punter steps up
and pulls it from her head

he wants the fantasy
she's not actually for sale,
wants to put her

through college.
There's something to be learned
from this woman—

buzz cut and cherry bomb
scalp tattoo—who looks him
dead in the eye, laughs.

Dewey Fox

Till You See a Street You Know

> *Is life, then, a dying by degrees? A sophism—an*
> *inadmissible and "venerable sophism." In this normal,*
> *hearty moment there is not even a particle of death . . . Let*
> *us conclude in the simplest and most elementary way*
> *possible: life is life and death is death.*
>   *—Jorge Guillen*

Getting here I went through the neighborhood we once found ourselves lost
in, when we didn't know the city & loved getting lost. You said: *Drive till*
you see a street you know & take it. Then it's a coin flip—headed home or the
wrong way. We passed a man who made a shooing motion at us with his hand
& thought he meant *You don't belong here*, found out years later that that's
the city's signal for *I'll pay you if you take me where I want to go*. You make
the same gesture now with the hand you can move, toward the window, or
the corner, or the blinds, or the chair by the window. I can't tell which, &
when I ask you slap the hand on your bed & say *Don't know*. It's gone, I
know, whatever you were asking for. A nurse floats in & wipes the tapioca off
your face, doesn't say a word to me. What you said about coin flips isn't any
truer now than then. Nothing's Manichean—not the avenues, not our cells.
Things go sideways a hundred different ways. It's a few days into a new year,
it's freezing & bright—just like then. When it started to come back, you said
Imagine you kicked Death off the rope ladder. You climb into the helicopter &
think you're flying home. Then the pilot turns around & it's Death. Big laughs.
You don't belong here. I'll pay you whatever you want if you can tell me what
I wanted. The nurse comes back & snaps the shades shut. *Michael likes to sleep*
around now, & I think the sun was getting in his eyes.

—Nominated by the Ohio University PhD Program in Creative Writing

Ashley Wang

God and I Play Russian Roulette / In Which the Youth Group Debates the Biblical Validity of Capital Punishment

The first scene of rapture opens like this: the glass
on my desk choking out a bullet, metal conception.
& suddenly you're barreling over my lampshade-
shadow-trapdoors, muzzle pulsing against
my temple. So I hollow. I swallow commas. I follow
you into a blank-spaced cellar, shatter the walls
with voids. & when the silence grows too wide, jams
against the spinning cylinder, I hand you a return
receipt with all the letters that slipped out the hatchway
of my belief. But let's reverse the roles, God. God,
your chamber's empty. God, don't bluff. Don't you see
the pistol in my palms, the way it blinks in this bonewhite
basement. So confess to me. Tell me, God. Tell
me the girl wasn't a blood lunar eclipse, fire-alarm hands
flitting over my jaw. How she wasn't an omen or another
ghost hanging from the ceiling. Tell me retribution isn't just
the way the moonlight bares its teeth over our license
plates each night. That the neon billboards hailing repent
or choose life won't haunt us down in a Kowloon pawn
shop tomorrow. Tell me this world will last. That we'll
be gorgeous for longer than five years, and we'll outlive
the trigger, and one day all there is to do is laugh
in the face of a picket sign. Tell me that language
isn't just a ship with interchangeable parts. It's okay,
keep talking. We both need this gunpoint to survive.
I already know the ivory church pews are just boneless

reproductions—discount doors to an empty Garden
of Eden. I've known for years that the girl's clasped
palms contain the entire sky. & wind is just another
verb for desire: her body split between the two parting
hands of a pocket watch, humming along the razor edge
of a 24-hour asymptote. See, I've been trying, God.
I've been trying to understand. When I first loved
the girl, I thought it final: we'd end as two pistols
baptized in a basement, caking gunpowder on
a country-fair mirror maze. Violent from all angles.
I, both the perpetrator and victim of my most
stunning crime, circumscribed by the reflections
of our slippery vocabularies. God, be honest—
here's my gun to the night and no more metaphors
to spill—tell me if a body like mine can live without
possession. Without ruin, without touch, without
light. Tell me a body like mine can pull the trigger
and still die holy.

Olivia McClure
Something About Me

Something about me reminds men of their daughters
and I say that because it's been said more than once
by more than one man on totally separate occasions
but I can only remember one instance well enough
it was the last year of middle school the same year
everything went to shit and by everything I mean all
my friends started cutting their legs and the first time
I saw it up close I gasped then apologized because I was
no stranger to watching someone punish themselves
but had never seen an entire leg beat up like that so sorry
for reacting I know it's rude to react but honestly when I
started hurting myself to fit in and because it's just
what you did when you were sad all I wanted was for
someone to react so I switched from my thigh to my wrist
and wore sleeves long enough to cover it when I was around
people I didn't care about but short enough to hike up
when I was around people I did and there were a few times
I let it show in homeroom because I saw this teacher
comfort a girl who stopped eating when she was sitting
outside the nurse's office and he looked like he really cared
and I wanted to be cared for too so I'd raise my hand
and let my sleeve fall and I know he must've seen it
I know other people did because one time a girl I hardly knew
and did not like told my best friend that she was letting me
kill myself and I called her a bitch because it wasn't
my best friend's fault and I didn't want to kill myself I just
wanted someone to tell me something nice and I'd hoped

it'd be a man because my father rarely called and when he did
it was never nice so I'd hoped my homeroom teacher would
step in but he didn't and when I stopped trying to get anyone's
attention and went back to my thighs he went off in the middle
of class and he was the type to get angry over nothing and
for some reason he didn't like me that day so when I laughed
at my best friend's doodle he stopped class and yelled in front
of everyone that I was a little brat and had a smartass look
on my face and I didn't know what to say except nothing
and sorry and no one knew what to say so class went back
to normal and a few days later he called me over to his desk
and told me he was sorry and said he was having a hard time
and reminded me that his kids lived in Florida with his ex-wife
and we were in Georgia and he missed his kids and rarely
got to see them and he was sorry for taking that out on me but
there was something about me that reminded him of his daughter.

—Nominated by the University of Maryland MFA Program in Creative Writing

Lachlan Chu
American Love Song

For the tiger, alone in the dying field
by the backyard fence, quiet
& so still
I had almost no reason
to hate him.
On his back,
through the branches, five gashes
of moonlight.
Again & again, he spoke
without a jaw: *you*
are nothing, you
are nothing.
Yes, I begged for language—
for a word
that meant I was not
still a boy, begging
for language.
Because here, in the dying field
with nothing else alive,
this was everything.
I was nothing.
I stood & watched the tiger:
his gorgeous eyes,
golden, sloshing in their sockets.
Two windows
where on the other side
there was a boy my age

with no symmetry,
a stone in one palm,
a world in the other.
An essay
in the double amber—*you
are nothing,*
you were the taste of
the pretty boy next door—*you,
tiger with no jaw,*
you were the mirror
& the rock—
*& I'm sorry
for all your hunger*
in this house
full of bread.

Phil SaintDenisSanchez

land back on Tchoupitoulas* (no one else can bring my music)

i burn an L gliding down Tchoupitoulas
    smoke trails linger on the past
        even if the Gulf rises and swallows the whole city to the hilt
          these streets can't be unnamed
        like spells bound to the wind beneath the wind—
          the wind that drives the wind & makes it howl

abandoned & abandoned & abandoned again
    in quiet ways like the Chapitoulas, in more ways like the wind, i
    still have breath & a voice
    still i can cascade a cataclysm from the clouds
        it's always raining when i leave New Orleans

let me show you the power of these ancient words
    krewe of Choctaw, krewe of Tchefuncte
    i can shout down heaven from a float
    sha the banter we on
    where y'at on Choctaw, Caddo land?
    dancing on broken-treaty'd concrete
        oak roots pumped thick through the sidewalk
        arcing justice into the second line

you can't speak of Louisiana's birth
without the Natchitoches words
    rolling lip-shaped breath into the mist

---

* Tchoupitoulas Street, named for the Chapitoulas tribe, who were one of the original inhabitants of the land that is now New Orleans.

i heard my seventh great calm the air in ceremony
drink the second cup
do what you came to do

Chief Big Leg, bless the medicine chalice
before i drink again
one thing about me
my ancestors don't play about me
you can test the waters
& be swept out to sea
like the French Navy trying to
hold onto Saint-Domingue
your stories & technology won't protect you

i was thinking about the stories
people must tell themselves to persist in their way
& how the stories keep them from seeing
what's already on its way back from the sky
keep them from
rolling back the time curtain
& hearing the reply
sung into the names
they say every day

what do you really know about these Tchoupitoulas blocks?
yeah, i know you know F & M Patio Bar at Lyons
where we used to have the Franklin reunions
whiskey-deep in spirits & unaware
drunk before the sunset
fully-dressed oyster po' boys at Domelise's
demanding our full attention
we'll destroy anything in our way to get them

the Tchoup Shop's windows smashed for the ATM once again
        what else did they expect?

côte des Chapitoulas
        some history books say the tribe is now extinct
but can't you taste the swell?
        hear heaven's shell start to crack
                in a triplet tap dance on the cobblestone
                        named for those who live by the river

god how they love the flow &
        how they rule this city
                in the dusted brass of Frenchmen,
                        the Quarter,
                                Tremé,
                        i hear the last laugh of a fate
                                decided by the disappeared
                my head bowed at Congo Square
                        i offer ceremonial tobacco to the grounds
                in exchange for dirt
        now on my altar
overcome with prayers for their return—

i had to lose everything to learn that nothing is ever lost

the moment i realized
        that i'd been heartbroken my whole life
                but so has everyone i've ever met
                        was the moment everything changed

the way fear always leads you back to itself
        if you ride it long enough
                it grows thick with night

it's always raining when i leave New Orleans
i let it kiss my face & promise return
knowing no one else can bring my music
land back must feel like falling in love

⊕

land back radiating from my limbs
            quiet prophecy burning in my thighs
land back in my sex
            feel it gathering lightning
                        for the spirits to ride
                                    back into the ground

land back like i can feel my marriage
            coming in slow motion
                        lilac & jasmine dreaming into
                                    the unconquistador'd air
land back a chant
            that becomes a vow
                        that has no choice but to happen
land back like falling in love
land back a heartbeat into the kingdom
land back humming heaven inside the whispered day
land back like falling in love
            earth & skin under-
                        wind aching for it
                                    the unconquistador'd air is ours

[To Coda ⊕ lighter on the return]

Audrey Rose

Variations on the Electric Slide

The artist, her body a statue
of wet clay in the small gray room,

said *boxes w/ light* & everyone
nodded & scribbled & nodded again,

but I heard *lightbox* I heard *father*
heard *cancer* heard mother repeat

his doctor back to me: *It's in his eyes*
& if it's in his eyes, it's in his brain

& if it's in his brain, it's in his spine
& in his blood & everywhere—

& everywhere, all at once, my father
entered the room. The light bulb

flashed the thin white palm
of its incandescent hand as he

waved *hello*—yes light is a particle
& a wave that my father uses

to wave hello or make a song
of his hands & flip me the bird

when I talk trash about him. No, he
wasn't skinny but he shimmy-flickered

himself electric & slid through the slender
vein of wires from one bulb to another—

you can't see it, you gotta feel it—
a silly jig he did behind the artist

as she went on to say something
important about life & art & signs

& that once you start noticing them
you'll find them all at once, everywhere.

This is an ekphrastic poem written after "Notations in Passing" in 2023, an art installation made of plywood, light bulbs, ceramic bases, and timers by Alicia Watkinson. Line twenty-three is an excerpt from "Electric Boogie (The Electric Slide)" by Marcia Griffiths.

Melissa Holm Shoemake
Self-Portrait in Haint Blue

I'm too young to understand
separation but my mother and I live
without my father

in an apartment full of crickets
and there's a dark cabinet
in my bedroom growing mold

I play games in, searching
for a talisman, creating
my own alchemy. I cast

myself as an ocean,
wish my being into a sky.

Some nights, my father comes
to me an apparition, slips
through paper thick cracks

in our foundation. I feign
sleep, feel a rough palm
stroke the curve of my golden

skull. He created
my breath to take it.

Our hours are restless
and in the chorus
of the sawed chirps

from the crickets her prayer
for protection to the Holy Spirit
becomes a refrain:

Cover us in the blood
of Jesus from the tops of our heads
to the soles of our feet.

Even then, I know something
of the future. My mother cannot suffer
the pulse my father summons

between her legs. He will needle
love into a bomb, eventually
strike her skin blue.

If faith is what makes
the supernatural true,

then I'm painting
myself indigo watered
down with my mother's milk.

Lis Sanchez

Carla Medina de Sánchez, August 23, 1899*:
Dark rags wing down

into the drowned sheepfold. Claws grip
the dead lamb as though its ribs were a raft
and they a dozen angels, storm wracked

and grunting strangled songs.   Up here,
in the ruptured church we women hunt
for sodden sticks, we strike them against

each other, watch them smolder inside
the cracked baptismal font. As though we had
one bone we could roast or suck dry.

As though we can't hear the plantations' agents
closing in—their drumming hooves, their rattling tins
of lucifers and crackers. Downhill, buzzards start

another bout of gag and hiss. Some give up
a grudging gap; the ugliest glare at
their neighbor's face and vomit. We turn

our cheeks and blow across the piled sticks,
we flap our hands. I circle the blasted cross, look for
something good to burn.

—Nominated by *The Fiddlehead*

---

* Fifteen days after landfall of San Ciriaco, the most destructive hurricane in Puerto Rico's history, and one day after landfall of a second hurricane.

Mary H. Lee
Good morning, I am forgetting

all the tulips and their delight. Every
       desire I find I take
an axe to. I shovel the flowers back
       into the earth. The typist
in my brain is punching away, saying
       mangoes! finches! a leaf! other
small miracles and for a moment
       I do, I almost believe
these words could be useful. These words
       which are not unlike the colorful
string of knotted scarves I once saw
       a magician pull from between
his teeth. How the unraveling seemed
       to go on forever. An easier trick:
one only needs to close both eyes.
       It's that simple. Everything
vanishes. *Goodbye*, I wave as I climb
       into a bed of moss, never to return.
The moss could become a hat,
       the hat could become a finch,
the finch could finally disappear.
       Yes, I can hear the birds sleeping,
opening themselves up to the night.
       No more of morning's
brightness ringing in my ears.

Divyasri Krishnan
Meditations in the Hottest Summer on Record

Let's go for a swim, I say, desperately
in love with you. A Wyoming sky
unfurls to an unseen point
beyond where light can touch. Before us,
a river dropped like a line of sapphires
into a cradle of peachleaf willows,
and my want, like a sister,
always a breath ahead.
You, undressed, the morning
light finding refuge in the down on your skin,
a golden shroud swallowed by the lip
of the river. You are half gone
to the water before I follow.
It is unseasonably warm. No shiver,
no bone-ache—the natural deterrents
erected by the world to make us think
twice about hasty love. A skin of silk
pulls up over the sensitive ankle,
the choral swell of the calf, into the eddy
behind the knee. What has already touched you
now touches me. And the heat
almost artificial, the result of years of longing
for comfort, a human sort of longing,
no respect for boundaries.
The salmon cannot abide this kind of heat.
They no longer disturb the river
with their chandeliers of light, their seeking,

their slender pumping muscles
shivering the world awake.
Their white, cooked bodies leave the low water.
Through the flute of love's vision they are
a hundred surfacing angels, a harbinger
of some distant dread, a haunt.
Who will witness us at the end, when we have wasted
the world to the fever of our want?

—Nominated by *Surging Tide Magazine*

Jamie L. Smith

In the Space between Pain

I.

Dirt cradles his heels. Bare-soled
my father treads the cold
grass each morning. A flood
of kerosine—

threads between
each bone, fire unleashed
with each step. The lit veins
race blitzkrieg beneath his skin.

He tells me, If this is all I get
it's been good. I want to believe him.
White goats pass where the pasture
dips low, bleat and hoofbeat

repeating. There's still
enough to live for,
he says, and I want to believe him.
Loons splash

the glacial lake
slow calling their hollow tune—
ripple and echo grown closer,
closer together, restless. I

am not ready for my father to die,
but I won't be angry—
not at him—
only at the goats, the loons, the sky

this fire
blazing him away.

II.

Advanced Directive:

I want to have
awareness of the past
and present, and hope

for the future,
my dad had written in.
We can't give him that,

the doctor says.
We're somewhere
in the dark field

between *poor*
and *futile* now. Lightning
strikes his body

every two
to three minutes—
convulsions the doctor says,

are

pure brainstem.

       I can do this,

I tell my stepmom,
who can't be there.

Are you sure?

       It's the last gift
       I'll get to give him.

III.

Lyric Time:

This might take some time,
sometimes a few hours, maybe

a couple days. When you enter
the Comfort Suite

it's understood you won't leave
until there's one

less person with you. Someone,
a clinical intern maybe,

in pale blue scrubs
and a rainbow lanyard

wheels a courtesy snack-cart
onto an elevator for you.

The poor woman arrives
smiling,

bearing her cookies, coffee
carafe, oranges,

and array of chips
as the doctor, stethoscope

against my father's chest
announces,

It's quiet inside.
Sometimes

it's seven minutes.

AJ White
Full Disclosure

Within the course of a few months, my calm, tall uncle
walked out into the pines, knelt down, & shot himself

in the chest—my titi drowned alone in her living room
in Little Havana, hundreds of cloth & ceramic cherubs

holding vigil from high cedar shelves around & above—
meanwhile in north Georgia my grandmother's mind at last

de-materialized across a barren, snow-kept causeway
onto a mineral sea, her eyes closed tight against the cold

passage, crying out in recognition,
from that place, of her own mother & father.

All recollection entails collection: autumn sun thins
like an old wound. Same year Benji swallowed his service

pistol. Same year dignity limped, finally, broken, wide
of my grasp. Holed up in motel rooms up & down

Appalachia, I drank as if I could preempt all my loves leaving
by ablation, sanding down the blade, dividing me by zero

& again. I survived, but left this outline there of my intent.
Some days the singe in my mouth of saltpeter & hickory coal

suggests I tread already as one of my own gone. Such proximity
is not unkind. Say that time & absence press by magnitude,

not, as we're told, by direction. There is no yet & past:
only gravities signaling I will see some of you soon.

A shocked dawn sears beneath the presidio
of my ribs. Say it will occur here.

—Nominated by Binghamton University Creative Writing Program

Marietta Brill
Sunflower Mandala

After Lewis Hyde

Have you noticed how many versions and revisions circulate the living air
Only the ghosts never leave

Your shambly gardens, mother loss, your one-way dialogues with trees
What is it with you and your obsession with leaves

Each sentence flowers, back to front and back again
Turning and turning for optimal sun exposure as it leaves

Images may be "beautiful" or "devastating"
Translucent against the sun, each approaches its own special value, leafily

There's variation in the number of ray-florets
Each line the sum of the one before, a spiral sequence of leaving

The friends who hold grieving within, the ones who leaf out
This world is too greenful for leaving

Have you ever seen such a bright planet
Appearing and disappearing through leaves

The *Melissodes trinodis* bee has a taste for sunflowers
Green eyes filled with golden angles of light and leaving

You once held your son in your palms like a seedling
Yet another metaphor about leaving

Beloved children and pets, shitty and good days, their green brightness
Mar, how will you fill your days before leaving

The last line holds a unique surface tension
A slant shadow beneath the leaves

Hannah Lee Nahar
Bricolage

An evening can be hole-shaped, lung-shaped, all clouds
and wire hoops jutting out from the garden. To be inattentive

to form requires an apathy I can't manage to summon, even in despair.
With arrows I diagram the sky: half blue, half storm. Like gray

matter imaged on any resonance machine, it's everywhere, the weather,
whose channel says it has begun to rain though we don't yet feel

any drops. False strawberries are bright spots here
and red there, tasting of nothing.

A branch sticks out for someone
to hold while pristine maggots feast on pristine apricots.

The first half of my diagram says PAY ATTENTION.
The second half, TO EVERYTHING. Even trying to catch

a break in sleep I'm an unchoosing witness to an image of me
running away from every shape I've ever seen.

Now, at the lake with no edges, our phones are so close to the shore
their digital clocks leap between time zones. Now, my knees sing

in the stretch-marked sand, scuffed from gathering purple
stones and the spiraling pasts trapped within them. I'm stung

by sand flies who did not name themselves
and I won't look at your private lighthouse.
You drew it with your hand.

If I could I would paint the page over as you did your old diary,
to protect it. Though years later I know you lifted its pigment

to the light to try and decode the veiled words.
By then it was all abstraction, all form, meaning buried

underneath. What you wanted, then not.
Pleasure, its little half loops—what I sought

was to go backwards. To unblow that dandelion.
For once to leave the wish whole instead of all in parts.

—Nominated by *Mississippi Review*

Danielle Weeks
Tun State

In the next life, I'll choose the tardigrade plan:
slow-stepping through lichen and moss, living
no longer than a human crush. My first love
was an entire planet that faded to a red-limned
speck in someone else's sky. Imagine how small
a loss would be to a body no bigger than one
millimeter, that has already survived all five
mass extinctions. I'm halfway there already:
curl into a ball at any small disaster, wander
always to the water for comfort, fill my cart
with plant-based goods. Come high radiation,
the sea-ice calving, deep space exploration—
come little body, move all the legs you have.

Acknowledgments

Dominique Ahkong's "Witch of the East" previously appeared in *Fugue*.

Marietta Brill's "Sunflower Mandala" previously appeared in *Radar Poetry*.

River 瑩瑩 Dandelion's "Ghazal Remix for Holy Summers" previously appeared in *Beloit Poetry Journal*.

Lachlan Chu's "American Love Song" previously appeared in *Poetry*.

Isabella DeSendi's "My Death Urge is Strong (Self-Portrait at Thirty)" previously appeared in *Brooklyn Poets*.

M.K. Foster's "Of the lights that goe before you" previously appeared in *The Gettysburg Review*.

Dewey Fox's "Till You See a Street You Know" previously appeared in *Northwest Review*.

Rob Greene's "To the Young Second Lieutenant Standing Behind Me in Line" previously appeared on *Poem-a-Day*.

Arielle Hebert's "Extra Life" previously appeared in *The Greensboro Review*.

Kaylee Young-Eun Jeong's "Last Spring" previously appeared in *ONLY POEMS*.

Mickie Kennedy's "Blue Collar" previously appeared in *The Southern Review*.

Divyasri Krishnan's "Meditations in the Hottest Summer on Record" previously appeared in *Surging Tide Magazine*.

Mary H. Lee's "Good morning, I am forgetting" previously appeared in *Blue Earth Review*.

Perry Levitch's "Leporiform" previously appeared in *Southeast Review*.

Shannan Mann's "A Bouquet of Lotuses for Your Birthday" previously appeared in *Going Down Swinging*.

Michael Mark's "Devotion" previously appeared in *Birmingham Poetry Review*.

Nathan Metz's "Fragment Sonnet" previously appeared in *The Santa Clara Review*.

Mia Nakaji Monnier's "Where I'm From" previously appeared in *parts:whole*.

Rachel Morgan's "Motherless Afternoon" previously appeared in *Beloit Poetry Journal*.

Hannah Lee Nahar's "Bricolage" previously appeared in *Mississippi Review*.

Andrew Navarro's "Heroes, Villains, Clouds" previously appeared in *Shenandoah*.

Sharon Pretti's "Waterline" previously appeared in *The MacGuffin*.

Audrey Rose's "Variations on the Electric Slide" previously appeared in *Good River Review*.

Lis Sanchez's "Carla Medina de Cienfuegos, August 23, 1899: Dark rags wing down" previously appeared in *The Fiddlehead*.

Melissa Holm Shoemake's "Self-Portrait in Haint Blue" previously appeared in *Iron Horse Literary Review*.

Jaz Sufi's "Magic Trick" previously appeared in *The Cortland Review*.

Avia Tadmor's "My Grandfather Delivers a Survivor's Testimony at Yad Vashem" previously appeared in *Narrative Magazine*.

Ashley Wang's "God and I Play Russian Roulette" previously appeared in *Black Warrior Review*.

Ann Weil's "Moon Child" previously appeared in *Burningword Literary Journal*.

AJ White's "Full Disclosure" previously appeared in *Fugue*.

Andrew Chi Keong Yim's "On Day One, I Quit" previously appeared in *Washington Square Review*.

Contributors' Notes

Dominique Ahkong is an Arizona-based poet of Hakka-Mauritian descent. Her work appears or is forthcoming in *The Southern Review*, *The Cincinnati Review*, *Cherry Tree*, *The Georgia Review*, and elsewhere. She was a finalist for the 2024 Slapering Hol Chapbook Contest. She co-edits *Shō Poetry Journal*. More at dominiqueahkong.com or @domkeykong.

Sherah Bloor is a South African poet and scholar. Her first collection, *The Gathering*, is forthcoming from Omnidawn in fall 2026, and she is currently working on a second book, tentatively titled *Archives of the Free World*. Sherah is also the editor and translator, with Tayseer Abu Odeh, of an anthology of recent poetry from Gaza and the West Bank, *You Must Live*, which will be published by Copper Canyon Press in fall 2025. She is completing a doctorate in philosophy of religion on the medical history of mental images at Harvard University, where she is the editor-in-chief of the literary and arts journal *Peripheries: A Journal of Word, Image, and Sound* (Harvard University Press). Her poems have appeared in *Chicago Review*, *Colorado Review*, *Conjunctions*, *Dialogist*, *Lana Turner*, and *Paperbark*, among other magazines.

Marietta Brill is the author of *I Stay Inside: A Crown of Sonnets* (The Grenfell Press). Her poems and other work can be found in *wildness*, *The Los Angeles Review*, *Thrush Poetry Journal*, hyperallergic.com, *Radar Poetry* (Coniston Finalist), *The Brooklyn Rail*, *Interim Poetics*, and more. She lives on the edge of a forest in New York's Catskill Mountains.

Jiordan Castle is the author of *Disappearing Act*, a memoir in verse. Her writing appears in *The New Yorker*, *The Rumpus*, *The Millions*, and elsewhere, including the anthology *What My Father and I Don't Talk About* (2025). She received her MFA in poetry from Hunter College and now lives in Philadelphia with her husband and their dog.

Lachlan Chu is a student at Columbia University and author of *Colossus in the Middle of Nowhere* (Bottlecap Press, 2024). His poems have previously appeared in *Poetry*, *diode*, and *The Harvard Advocate*.

LAUREN CRAWFORD earned an MFA in poetry from Southern Illinois University, Carbondale. A native of Houston, Texas, she is the recipient of the 2023 Willie Morris Award. Her debut collection, *Catch & Release*, is forthcoming in spring 2025 with Cornerstone Press as part of the Portage Poetry Series. Her poetry has either appeared or is forthcoming in *Poet Lore, Passengers Journal, Prime Number Magazine, SoFloPoJo, The Florida Review, Red Ogre Review, Ponder Review, The Midwest Quarterly, THIMBLE, The Worcester Review, The Spectacle*, and elsewhere. Lauren teaches writing at the University of New Haven and serves on the editorial teams of Iron Oak Editions, *Palette Poetry*, and *Alan Squire Publishing Bulletin*.

BERTHA ISABEL Crombet was born in Santiago, Cuba, but lived in Miami for twenty-one years, where she received her MFA in poetry from Florida International University. She has been published in *Jai-Alai Magazine, Black Warrior Review, New Delta Review*, and others. Most recently, she earned her PhD in creative writing at Florida State University.

RIVER 瑩瑩 Dandelion (he, him, keoi 佢) walks with his ancestors. He is a practitioner of ancestral medicine through writing, teaching, energy healing, and creating ceremony. Winner of the 2024 Lambda Literary Award for Exceptional New LGBTQ Writers, River is the author of *remembering (y)our light*, a debut chapbook on honoring matriarchs and ancestors across generations. He has been awarded residencies and fellowships from Baldwin for the Arts, Bread Loaf, Caldera Arts, Headlands Center for the Arts, Tin House, Vermont Studio Center, and more. River loves to swim and does this work for queer and trans ancestors and descendants to come. To connect, visit riverdandelion.com.

EMMA DePANISE is a poet from the Eastern Shore of Maryland. Her poems have appeared in venues such as *Poetry Northwest, The Minnesota Review, Verse Daily, The National Poetry Review*, and others. She holds an MFA from Purdue University and is a current PhD student in creative writing at the University of Missouri.

ISABELLA DeSENDI is a Latina poet and educator whose work is published or is forthcoming in *Poetry, The Adroit Journal, Poetry Northwest*, and others. Her debut poetry collection titled *Someone Else's Hunger* will be published by Four Way Books in 2025. Her chapbook *Through the New Body* won the Poetry Society of America's Chapbook Fellowship and was published in 2020. Recently, she received a *Poets & Writers* BIPOC grant, has been named a finalist for the Rattle Poetry Prize, *Frontier*'s Digital Poetry Chapbook Prize, the June Jordan Fellowship, *Narrative Magazine*'s Annual Poetry Prize, and *Palette*'s Spotlight Award. She has attended Bread Loaf Writers' Workshop and will soon attend the Storyknife Writers' Residency in Alaska. Isabella holds an MFA from Columbia University and currently lives in Hoboken, New Jersey.

GABRIEL FINE is a writer from Colorado. His poetry appears in *Gulf Coast*, *Missouri Review*, and other journals, and he has published nonfiction in outlets like the *Texas Observer* and *Los Angeles Review of Books*. He received an MFA from the Michener Center for Writers.

M.K. FOSTER is a poet, gothic fiction writer, historian of science, and public storyteller from Alabama. Her work has appeared or is forthcoming in *The American Poetry Review*, *Nimrod*, *The Gettysburg Review*, *Kenyon Review*, and elsewhere, and she has presented her archival research on Renaissance monstrosity, sharks, and apocalypses at the Newberry Library, the National Museum of Denmark, and elsewhere. In 2024, she was named a MacDowell Fellow in Literature and selected for the Fulbright US Scholar Award in Creative Writing to Queens University Belfast. Foster holds an MFA and a PhD, but holds especially dear her work as a bookseller and storytime lady at Little Professor Books in Birmingham, Alabama. For writings, sharks, monsters, and more, please visit marykatherinefoster.com.

DEWEY FOX is from Perryville, Maryland. He received an MFA in poetry from the University of Oregon and is a PhD candidate in creative writing at Ohio University. His work has appeared in *Poet Lore* and *Northwest Review*.

ROB GREENE is the founder and publisher of *Raleigh Review*, and he is a father of four. A former Virginia Center for the Creative Arts fellow, he was also a Weymouth Center Writer-in-Residence. Greene received his PhD from University of Birmingham in England and his MFA in creative writing from North Carolina State University.

ARIELLE HEBERT is a queer poet based in North Carolina with roots in Florida and Louisiana. She holds an MFA in poetry from North Carolina State University. She won the 2024 Lit/South Award for Poetry selected by Jericho Brown. Her work has appeared or is forthcoming in *Southern Humanities Review*, *Grist*, *Great River Review*, *Nimrod*, *Willow Springs*, and *Redivider*, among others. Arielle believes in ghosts and magic. www.ariellehebert.com.

PERRY JANES is the author of the recent poetry collection *Find Me When You're Ready* (Northwestern University Press/Curbstone Books). A recipient of the Pushcart Prize, his work has appeared or is forthcoming in *Poetry*, *Electric Literature*, *Poem-a-Day*, *Zyzzyva*, *Threepenny Review*, and elsewhere. He holds a BA from the University of Michigan, where he was a five-time recipient of The Hopwood Award, and an MFA in poetry from Warren Wilson College. Originally from metro Detroit, Michigan, he lives in California, where he works as a screenwriter.

KAYLEE YOUNG-EUN JEONG is from Oregon. A 2024 Tahoma Literary Review Fellow at the Mineral School Artist Residency, her work can be found in *The Adroit Journal*, *ONLY POEMS*, *Shenandoah*, and *Tinderbox*, among others. She unconditionally supports the liberation of Palestine and Palestinian people.

KARAN KAPOOR is the editor-in-chief of *ONLY POEMS*. A finalist for the *Diode*, *Tusculum Review*, and *Iron Horse Literary Review* chapbook prizes, their poems appear or are forthcoming in *AGNI*, *Shenandoah*, *Colorado Review*, *Cincinnati Review*, *North American Review*, and elsewhere, fiction in *JOYLAND* and *the other side of hope*, and translations in *The Offing* and *The Los Angeles Review*. They're on the editorial board of Alice James Books.

MICKIE KENNEDY is a gay writer who resides in Baltimore County, Maryland. His work has appeared or is forthcoming in *Poetry*, *The Threepenny Review*, *The Southern Review*, *The Sun*, and elsewhere. Follow him on X/Instagram @MickiePoet or his website at mickiekennedy.com.

CHRIS KETCHUM is from Moscow, Idaho. He received an MFA from Vanderbilt University. A doctoral candidate at Georgia State University, he works as an editor of *Beyond Bars*, a literary magazine that publishes poetry and prose by writers impacted by the carceral system. His poems have appeared in *Beloit Poetry Journal*, *Copper Nickel*, *Missouri Review*'s Poem of the Week, and elsewhere.

Divyasri Krishnan is a writer from Massachusetts. Her work appears in *DIAGRAM*, *Frontier Poetry*, *Muzzle Magazine*, and elsewhere. She has further been recognized by the Kenyon Review Writers Workshop, the Pittsburgh Humanities Festival, and the Periplus Fellowship.

Mary H. Lee received her MFA in poetry from the University of Texas at Austin, where she was a James A. Michener Fellow. Her poems can be found in *New England Review* and *Blue Earth Review*. She lives and writes in Phoenix.

Perry Levitch's poems have appeared in the *New England Review*, the *Southeast Review*, the *Columbia Review*, and others. They are a Best of the Net and Pushcart Prize nominee. They received an MFA from NYU, where they were poetry editor of *Washington Square Review*. Currently, they are studying transpoetics as a PhD student at Brown.

Shannan Mann is the founding editor of *ONLY POEMS*. She has been awarded or placed for the Palette Love & Eros Prize, Rattle Poetry Prize, Auburn Witness Prize, and the Foster Poetry Prize, among others. Her poems appear in *Poetry Daily*, *Black Warrior Review*, *Missouri Review*, *Poet Lore*, *Gulf Coast*, *The Literary Review of Canada*, *EPOCH*, *december*, and elsewhere. She is the poet laureate's pick for *Exile*. Her essays appear in *Tolka Journal* and *Going Down Swinging*; they have been awarded the Alta Lind Cook Prize and the Irene Adler Essay Prize. She also translates Sanskrit poetry.

Michael Mark takes long walks to help him write. He's trekked the Himalayas, and completed the Camino De Santiago three times. His chapbook, *Visiting Her in Queens Is More Enlightening than a Month in a Monastery in Tibet*, won the Rattle Chapbook Prize. His poems appear in *Alaska Quarterly Review*, *Copper Nickel*, *New Ohio Review*, *Ploughshares*, *Southern Review*, *The Sun*, *32 Poems*, and the Poetry Foundation's *American Life in Poetry*. Find him at michaeljmark.com.

Olivia McClure is a second-year poet and graduate teaching assistant in the University of Maryland's MFA program in creative writing. She earned her BA in English from Georgia College and State University in Milledgeville, Georgia. Olivia is a reader for *Frontier Poetry*, and her poems have appeared in *Atticus Review* and *Atlanta Review*.

NATHAN METZ (he/his) is a writer and teacher from California. His work has been featured in *Autofocus*, *The Racket*, and elsewhere. He is an MFA candidate at the University of Illinois Urbana–Champaign.

MIA NAKAJI MONNIER is a writer in Los Angeles. Her writing has been featured in *The Boston Globe*, *BuzzFeed News*, KCET, *Los Angeles Review of Books*, *Shondaland*, *The Washington Post*, and the book *This Long Thread: Women of Color on Craft, Community, and Connection* by Jen Hewett (Roost Books, 2022), among other publications. She has worked as an editor at *Guernica*, *Hunker*, *Apartment Therapy*, *HelloGiggles*, and the Japanese American community newspaper *The Rafu Shimpo*.

RACHEL MORGAN is a 2024 Iowa Artist Fellow, and her work recently appears in *Prairie Schooner*, *Alaska Quarterly Review*, *JAMA*, *Notre Dame Review*, and *Shenandoah*. She is the winner of the 2020 Fineline Competition and a recent finalist in the National Poetry Series. She is a graduate of the Iowa Writers' Workshop and teaches at the University of Northern Iowa. She is an editor for *North American Review*.

HANNAH LEE Nahar is a writer, interdisciplinary artist, and educator. Their poems appear in journals such as *West Branch*, *Salt Hill*, *Passages North*, and *Mississippi Review*. Hannah completed an MFA in poetry at The Ohio State University, where they taught creative writing to students of all ages and acted in various editorial roles for *The Journal*. They grew up in the Boston area and now live in Brooklyn.

ANDREW NAVARRO lives in California where he teaches world history in the city of Moreno Valley. His poetry has been published in journals such as *Poet Lore*, *Michigan Quarterly Review*, and *Zyzzyva*. He holds degrees in English and creative writing from California State University, San Bernardino, and the University of California, Riverside.

FIKER GIRMA NEGASH is a development economics researcher at Princeton University. She is a recipient of the Roger Conant Hatch Prize for Lyric Poetry and finalist in the Adroit Prizes for Poetry and Prose. She is from Addis Ababa, Ethiopia.

MICHAEL O'RYAN's poems appear or are forthcoming in *Narrative Magazine, Ninth Letter, The Greensboro Review, Third Coast*, and elsewhere. A finalist for American Literary Review's Poetry Award, *New Letters'* Patricia Cleary Miller Award, and *Narrative's* Annual Poetry Prize, he holds an MFA from the Helen Zell Writers' Program at the University of Michigan, where he won a Hopwood Award and received a Zell Postgraduate Fellowship.

CASEY PATRICK's poetry appears in *The Massachusetts Review, Pleiades, Radar Poetry, The Adroit Journal*, and elsewhere. She has an MFA from Eastern Washington University and has received fellowships and grants from Vermont Studio Center, Hub City Writers Project, and the Minnesota State Arts Board. She lives in Minneapolis.

SHARON PRETTI lives in San Francisco, California. Her work has appeared in numerous journals including *Calyx, The MacGuffin, Spillway, The Bellevue Literary Review*, and *Canary*. She has received multiple Pushcart Prize nominations. She is also an award-winning haiku poet and frequent contributor to haiku journals including *Modern Haiku* and *Frogpond*. Sharon is a retired medical social worker and, for many years, she had the pleasure of teaching poetry workshops in a nursing home and at assisted living facilities in the San Francisco Bay Area. Her website is sharonpretti.com.

AUDREY ROSE earned her BA in mathematics and completed her MFA in creative writing at the University of South Florida (USF). She has guest lectured at USF and served as an art and poetry editor for *Saw Palm: Florida Literature and Art*. Her work has been nominated for a Pushcart Prize, and her poetry appears in *SLAB, Sweet Lit, Arts Coast, Halfway Down the Stairs, Good River Review, Epiphany*, and *Poetry*.

PHIL SAINTDENISSANCHEZ is a Creole poet from New Orleans. His work has appeared or is forthcoming in *Poetry International, Tinderbox Poetry Journal*, and elsewhere. He was a finalist for *Poetry International's* C.P. Cavafy Prize as well as a finalist for *The Atlas Review's* and *Button Poetry's* chapbook contests, and a notable manuscript for *BOAAT's* chapbook contest. A semifinalist for the 2020 Discovery Prize, he has received scholarships to attend Bread Loaf Writers' Conference and presented at AWP on creating collaborations between poetry and music. His debut collection, *before & after our bodies*, is forthcoming on Button

Poetry in 2025. He studied music theory and composition at The City College of New York, records under the name SaintDenisSanchez, and currently lives in Brooklyn.

LIS SANCHEZ is a grateful recipient of a North Carolina Artist Fellowship. Her poems appear in *The Fiddlehead, Poetry, The Bark, The Southern Review, The Georgia Review, Ploughshares*, and *Copper Nickel*. Her work has received literary awards from the editors of *Prairie Schooner, Nimrod, RHINO*, and *The Greensboro Review*.

DANIEL SCHONNING's poems have appeared in *Poetry, Poetry Daily, Orion Magazine, The Yale Review*, and elsewhere. A runner-up for 92NY's 2022 Discovery Poetry Contest, Schonning won both the 2023 Omnidawn Broadside Prize and *Crazyhorse*'s 2020 Lynda Hull Memorial Prize. He lives in Geneva, New York, where he teaches creative writing at Hobart and William Smith Colleges and serves as a poetry editor for *Seneca Review*.

MELISSA HOLM SHOEMAKE lives in Atlanta, Georgia, with her husband and two sons where she works in college administration at Emory University. She holds an MFA in poetry from the University of Mississippi and her poems have appeared in various journals and anthologies including *The Southern Humanities Review, The Shore, Harpur Palate, Iron Horse Literary Review*, and *The Southern Poetry Anthology*. Her chapbook, *Ab.Sin.The.*, is available from Dancing Girl Press.

JAMIE L. SMITH holds an MFA in creative writing from CUNY Hunter College and is a current PhD candidate in English literature and creative writing at the University of Utah. Her debut collection, *The Flightless Years*, is forthcoming from Finishing Line Press. Her chapbook *Mythology Lessons* was winner of Tusculum Review's 2020 Nonfiction Prize and is listed as notable in *Best American Essays 2021*. Her poetry, nonfiction, and hybrid works appear in publications including *Southern Humanities Review, Bellevue Literary Review, The Write Launch, Red Noise Collective*, and anthologies by *Indi(e) Blue, Allegory Ridge*, and *Beyond Queer Words*. Please visit jlsmithwriter.com for more information.

JAZ SUFI (she/hers) is a queer Iranian-American poet and arts educator. Her work has been published or is upcoming in *Best of the Net, AGNI, Black Warrior Review, Muzzle*, and elsewhere. She is a National Poetry Slam finalist and has received fellowships from

Kundiman, the Watering Hole, and New York University, where she received her MFA. She is the current poet laureate of San Ramon, California, where she lives with her dog, Apollo.

Avia Tadmor's poetry collection, *Song in Tammuz*, has won the Tupelo Press International Berkshire Prize and is forthcoming in 2026. Avia's poems appear or are forthcoming in *The New Republic*, *New England Review*, *Prairie Schooner*, and elsewhere. Her poetry received fellowships from Yaddo, the Rona Jaffe Foundation/Bread Loaf, the Vermont Studio Center, the Virginia Center for the Creative Arts, and the *Adroit Journal*'s Gregory Djanikian Scholars Program. Avia teaches writing at New York University.

Ashley Wang lives between New Haven, Connecticut, and Hong Kong. Her work has been published in *Waxwing*, *Black Warrior Review*, *Dialogist*, *Gigantic Sequins*, and elsewhere. She is a sophomore at Yale, where she performs spoken word about *The Matrix* and desire with WORD.

Danielle Weeks earned her MFA in poetry through Eastern Washington University's creative writing program. Her poetry has been published or is forthcoming in *The Missouri Review*, *Pleiades*, and *Whale Road Review*, among others. Her poem "Human Uses" was chosen as the winner of *Atticus Review*'s annual poetry contest in 2018, and her poetry manuscript was a finalist for the 2023 Charles B. Wheeler Poetry Prize. She is a poetry editor for *Crab Creek Review*.

Ann Weil is the author of *Lifecycle of a Beautiful Woman* (Yellow Arrow Publishing, 2023) and *Blue Dog Road Trip* (Gnashing Teeth Publishing, 2024). Nominated for the Pushcart Prize and Best of the Net, her poetry appears in *Pedestal Magazine*, *DMQ Review*, *Maudlin House*, *3Elements Review*, *Chestnut Review*, and elsewhere. She divides her time between Ann Arbor, Michigan, and Key West, Florida.

Dylan Weir is a writer. He lives in Chicago with his wife and two children. His debut manuscript, *Public House*, has been named a finalist in a number of prizes. As of this writing, it is still available.

AJ White is a poet and educator from north Georgia. AJ's debut book, *Blue Loop*, was selected for the 2024 National Poetry Series by Chelsea Dingman and is forthcoming from University of Georgia Press fall 2025. AJ is also the winner of the 2023 Fugue Poetry Prize, selected by Kaveh Akbar, and of a 2023 Academy of American Poets University Prize, selected by Tara Betts. His work has appeared in *Overheard*, *Taco Bell Quarterly*, *West Trade Review*, and elsewhere. He teaches creative writing and lives in New York.

Carson Wolfe is a Mancunian poet and winner of *New Writing North*'s Debut Poetry Prize (2023). Their work has appeared with *Rattle*, *The Rumpus*, *The North*, *The Common*, and is forthcoming with *Poetry* magazine. They were longlisted in The Poetry Society's National Competition (2023), and have received awards from The Aurora Poetry Prize, The Edward Thomas Fellowship and Button Poetry. You can find them at carsonwolfe.co.uk.

Andrew Chi Keong Yim was born and raised in Honolulu, Hawai'i. He is the Martha Meier Renk Fellow at the University of Wisconsin–Madison, and was awarded the 2024 New Voices Award in Poetry from the *Washington Square Review*, selected by Terrance Hayes. His poetry has appeared or is forthcoming in AAWW's *The Margins*, and *Washington Square Review*. He has been a middle school English teacher in Boston and New York City, and currently teaches undergraduates at the University of Wisconsin–Madison and incarcerated writers through the Wisconsin Prison Humanities Project.

Participating Magazines

32 Poems
32poems.com

805 Lit + Art
805lit.org

Able Muse
ablemuse.com

The Account
theaccountmagazine.com

The Adroit Journal
theadroitjournal.org

AGNI
agnionline.bu.edu

ALOCASIA
alocasia.org

American Literary Review
americanliteraryreview.com

ANMLY
anmly.org

Apple Valley Review
applevalleyreview.com

ARTS & LETTERS
artsandletters.gcsu.edu

Barrelhouse
barrelhousemag.com

Bayou Magazine
bayoumagazine.org

Beestung
beestungmag.com

Bellevue Literary Review
blreview.org

Bellingham Review
bhreview.org

Beloit Poetry Journal
bpj.org

Bennington Review
benningtonreview.org

Birmingham Poetry Review
uab.edu/cas/englishpublications/
    birmingham-poetry-review

Blackbird
blackbird.vcu.edu

Black Warrior Review
bwr.ua.edu

Bloodroot
bloodrootlit.org

Booth: A Journal
booth.butler.edu

Cagibi
cagibilit.com

Cherry Tree
washcoll.edu/cherrytree

Cincinnati Review
cincinnatireview.com

Copper Nickel
copper-nickel.org

Cutleaf
cutleafjournal.com

Diode
diodepoetry.com

DIALOGIST
dialogist.org

The Dodge
thedodgemag.com

Ecotone
ecotonemagazine.org

EVENT Magazine
eventmagazine.ca

The Fiddlehead
thefiddlehead.ca

Fjords Review
fjordsreview.com

The Florida Review
floridareview.cah.ucf.edu

Foglifter
foglifterjournal.com

Free State Review
freestatereview.com

Frozen Sea
frozensea.org

Fugue
fuguejournal.com

The Georgia Review
thegeorgiareview.com

The Good Life Review
thegoodlifereview.com

Greensboro Review
greensbororeview.org

Hamilton Arts & Letters
HALmagazine.com

Hayden's Ferry Review
haydensferryreview.com

Hominum
hominumjournal.org

Honey Literary
honeyliterary.com

The Hopkins Review
hopkinsreview.com

After Happy Hour Review
afterhappyhourreview.com

Image
imagejournal.org

Iris
iris.virginia.edu

Iron Horse
ironhorsereview.com

Jet Fuel Review
jetfuelreview.com

The Journal
english.osu.edu/mfa

The Lascaux Review
lascauxreview.com

Lucky Jefferson
luckyjefferson.com

The MacGuffin
schoolcraft.edu/macguffin

The Margins
aaww.org

The McNeese Review
mcneese.edu/thereview

Michigan Quarterly Review
sites.lsa.umich.edu/mqr

Mid-American Review
casit.bgsu.edu/midamericanreview

Minyan Magazine
minyanmag.com

Mississippi Review
www.mississippireview.com

MORIA Literary Magazine
moriaonline.com

Muzzle Magazine
muzzlemagazine.com

New England Review
nereview.com

Newfound
newfound.org

New Orleans Review
neworleansreview.org

The Night Heron Barks
nightheronbarks.com

Nimrod International Journal
artsandsciences.utulsa.edu/nimrod/

Ninth Letter
ninthletter.com

Okay Donkey
okaydonkeymag.com

Passages North
passagesnorth.com

Phoebe
phoebejournal.com

Ploughshares
pshares.org

The Pinch
pinchjournal.com

Poem-A-Day
poets.org/poem-day

Poet Lore
poetlore.com

$ - Poetry Is Currency
poetrycurrency.com

Posit Journal
positjournal.com

Prism Review
sites.laverne.edu/prism-review

PRISM International
prismmagazine.ca

Psaltery & Lyre
psalteryandlyre.org

Quarterly West
quarterlywest.com

Radar Poetry
radarpoetry.com

Radon Journal
radonjournal.com

Raleigh Review
RaleighReview.org

Rat's Ass Review
ratsassreview.net

River Styx
riverstyx.org

Room Magazine
roommagazine.com

Salamander
salamandermag.org

The Santa Clara Review
santaclarareview.com

Sapiens
sapiens.org

Sewanee Review
thesewaneereview.com

Shenandoah
shenandoahliterary.org

Sho Poetry Journal
shopoetryjournal.com

Sine Theta Magazine
sinetheta.net

Slab
slablitmag.org

Slippery Elm
slipperyelm.findlay.edu

The Southeast Review
southeastreview.org

The Southern Review
thesouthernreview.org

The Spectacle
thespectacle.wustl.edu

Split Lip Magazine
splitlipthemag.com

Sugar House Review
SugarHouseReview.com

Surging Tide
surgingtidemag.com

swamp pink
swamp-pink.cofc.edu

SWWIM Every Day
swwim.org

Tahoma Literary Review
tahomaliteraryreview.com

Terrain
terrain.org

Third Coast
thirdcoastmagazine.com

Thrush Poetry Journal
thrushpoetryjournal.com

Up the Staircase Quarterly
upthestaircase.org

Virginia Quarterly Review
vqronline.org

Washington Square Review
washingtonsquarereview.com

Waxwing Literary Journal
waxwingmag.org

Whale Road Review
whaleroadreview.com

wildness
readwildness.com

Witness
witness.blackmountaininstitute.org

Zaum
zaum.sonoma.edu

ZYZZYVA
zyzzyva.org

Participating Programs

American University Creative Writing Program
american.edu/cas/literature/mfa

College of Charleson MFA in Creative Writing
english.cofc.edu/graduate-programs/master-fine-arts-creative-writing

Florida International University MFA in Creative Writing
english.fiu.edu/creative-writing

Florida State University Creative Writing
english.fsu.edu/programs/creative-writing

Hollins University Jackson Center for Creative Writing
hollinsmfa.wordpress.com

Johns Hopkins The Writing Seminars
writingseminars.jhu.edu

McNeese State University MFA Program
mfa.mcneese.edu

Miami Univerisity Creative Writing MFA
miamioh.edu/cas/academics/departments/english/academics/graduate-studies/creative-writing/
    residential-mfa

Minnesota State University Mankato Creative Writing Program
english.mnsu.edu/cw

New Mexico State University MFA in Creative Writing
english.nmsu.edu/graduate-programs/mfa

New School Writing Program
newschool.edu/writing

New York University Creative Writing Program
as.nyu.edu/cwp

Northwestern University MA/MFA in Creative Writing
sps.northwestern.edu/program-areas/graduate/creative-writing

The Ohio State University MFA Program in Creative Writing
english.osu.edu/mfa

Ohio University Creative Writing PhD
ohio.edu/cas/english/grad/creative-writing/index.cfm

Southeast Missouri State University Master of Arts in English
semo.edu/english

SUNY Birmingham Creative Writing Program
binghamton.edu/english/creative-writing

Syracuse University MFA in Creative Writing
english.syr.edu/cw/cw-program.html

Texas Tech University Creative Writing Program
depts.ttu.edu/english/cw

UMass Amherst MFA for Poets and Writers
umass.edu/englishmfa

UMass Boston MFA Program in Creative Writing
umb.edu/academics/cla/english/grad/mfa

UNC Greensboro Creative Writing Program
mfagreensboro.org

University of Tennessee MFA in Creative Writing
english.utk.edu/grad/mfa-creative.php

University of Alabama at Birmingham Graduate Theme in Creative Writing
uab.edu/cas/english/graduate-program/creative-writing

University of Idaho MFA in Creative Writing
uidaho.edu/class/english/graduate/mfa-creative-writing

University of Kansas Graduate Creative Writing Program
englishcw.ku.edu

University of Maryland MFA Program
english.umd.edu

University of Missouri Creative Writing Program
english.missouri.edu/area/creative-writing

University of New Orleans Creative Writing Workshop
uno.edu/writing

University of North Texas Creative Writing
english.unt.edu/creative-writing-0

University of San Francisco MFA in Writing
usfca.edu/mfa

University of Southern Mississippi Center for Writers
usm.edi/writers

University of Texas Michener Center for Writers
michener.utexas.edu

University of Utah Creative Writing Program
english.utah.edu

Virginia Tech MFA in Creative Writing Program
liberalarts.vt.edu/departments-and-schools/department-of-english/academic-programs/master-of-fine-arts-in-creative-writing.html

Western Michigan University Creative Writing Program
wmich.edu/english

West Virginia University MFA Program
creativewriting.wvu.edu

The series editor wishes to thank the many poets involved in our first round of reading:

Caroline Erickson, Kate Coleman, ethan evans, max gregg, Kamau Walker, and Holly Zhou.

Special thanks to Jason Coleman and the University of Virginia Press for their editorial advice and support for this poetry project.